Bon Appétit! from the Restaurants of

PARK CITY

A Mountain Town's Cookbook

Enjoy a Taste of **PARK CITY** Restaurants
in Your Own Kitchen

Park City Publishing / Park City, Utah 2016

Dedication

I dedicated this book to my father, Arch Nadler, who inspired me and encouraged me throughout my life.
He introduced me to Park City in 1972 – a town that I quickly learned to love: the skiing,
streets and shops, the surrounding mountains, and the town's incredible restaurants.
To my son, Cameron, the best son a mother could hope for, who constantly exceeds my expectations.
And to my husband, Roger, for his constant love and support.

Introduction: Letter from Publisher

How could you not love this town? I first arrived in Park City with my family in 1972 to enjoy a few weeks of skiing, and then every year after that up to 1980 when I moved here to work for the resort in the typical fashion of a full time skier – all day on the slopes and then nighttime working in a restaurant. I spent the 1990's and 2000's back on the East Coast working as an art director for some of the world's top publishers and design studios, but made sure that I was back for at least a week or two for each ski season. 2010 saw us back in Park City for good to ski, hike, bike, and for me to continue my work as an art director and, more recently, as the publisher and creative director of Park City Publishing.

With this book I wanted to share some of the things that I love about Park City – of course I cannot share the experience of skiing, or biking, or the crisp mountain air, or the gentle breezes of summer, but I can share much of the town by way of some incredible photos. I can also share the tastes of Park City as many of the town's top restaurants have contributed recipes of some of their most prized dishes, so that an evening's dining experience at their restaurants can be created at home – wherever that home might be.

These recipes were contributed by 21 different establishments directly from each chef, in his or her own words. We have strived to make the recipes as consistent, clear, and 'home cook' friendly as possible.

So here's my gift to you, a true, 'taste', of Park City. Bon Appétit!

Acknowledgments

A huge thank you to all my friends and family, and to the restaurants and chefs of Park City who have contributed their recipes and stories and endured my repeated visits to collect all the information necessary to produce this book.

A special thank you to my husband Roger for putting aside his books to walk up and down main street with me to help recruit the participating restaurants. Further thanks to friends who have helped along the way.
Pam Archbold for being an amazing editor with her expertise of cooking and ability to make sense of the chefs' recipes.
Pat Cone for stepping in to interview the chefs and staff for the feature pages, for his food, restaurant, and Park City scenic photography.
My good friend Donna Sheeran, early on, to help recruit restaurants on board with this project.
And Phil Archbold for his beautiful secnic photography and giving up his wife for a week of intense editing.

CONTENTS
and Key Code

CV Canyons Village **DV** Deer Valley **K** Kamas **MS** Main Street **OM** Off Main Street **P** Prospector **SL** Silver Lake **SS** Silver Star

A Appetizer **S** Soup/Salad **E** Entrée **SD** Side Dish **D** Dessert

Contents con't

BON APPÉTIT
From the Restaurants of

PARK CITY

350 MAIN

MS

This is the finest of fine dining, in the largest historic building on Main Street, celebrating its 20th anniversary this year. You'll marvel over the original pressed tin ceiling in a room that once housed a food market, a nightclub, and was the predecessor to the J.C. Penney empire: The Golden Rule. These walls will speak to you as you dine, telling tales of Park City's past, while enjoying the elegant, muted ambience.

The menu reflects the times, with contemporary American cuisine. They keep things simple, classic, and fresh. Chef Safranek's creations are delicious, and gorgeous, using local and sustainable food sourced right here in the Wasatch Mountains.

Order the roasted Colorado elk sausage from the tapas menu at the bar, or a blue crab cake with Caribbean chutney, all while enjoying one of the signature martinis - perhaps the cinnamon snowball - or a High West Manhattan. Seated in front of the large front windows, or in the high-topped, cozy banquettes, you can watch the Park City promenade down Main Street.

Start your meal with a salad of organic greens with grilled peach, the PEI mussels with chorizo and foccacia, or the ever-popular tuna tower with wasabi cream and avocado. Then order the black sesame scallops for your main course, and be prepared to share: they're stupendous.

Or dig in to the crispy gluten-free fried chicken, marinated in buttermilk. It's almost too beautiful to eat...almost. Finish your dinner, and yourself, off with the tequila infused key lime pie, with toasted coconut and hibiscus sauce.

For special occasions and events you may reserve the Vintage Room, or dine on the Terrace in front of the large stone fireplace. The motto at 350 Main is simple: "Serve delicious, healthy food that guests will want to return to week after week."

Chef Matthew Safranek is meticulous as he prepares his award-winning dishes, whether the exact placement of the house-made bark on the key lime pie, or balancing the sweet potato garnish above the gluten-free chicken.

In his third season at 350 Main, Chef Safranek says he "loves the adrenaline rush of the dinner service," and the creativity involved in the kitchen.

He has previously cooked at the Tribeca Grill in New York, the Shelburne in Dublin, and Atria on Martha's Vineyard. He says one of the high points was working with Beard Award winner Jonathan Sundstrom in Seattle.

Chef Safranek says, "There's always something new to learn."

PG4   PG5   PG6   PG7

Tuna Tower with Wasabi Cream and Avocado

1½ lbs big eye or yellow fin tuna, diced
¼ avocado, diced
small sprouts or microgreens for garnish

CORN STARCH SLURRY
3 Tbsp corn starch and ¼ cup water

WASABI AIOLI
¼ cup mayonnaise
1 Tbsp sour cream
¾ tsp wasabi powder
¼ tsp lemon juice

MARINADE
2 Tbsp sweet thai chili sauce
2 Tbsp soy sauce
1 Tbsp fresh lime juice
1 Tbsp fresh lemon juice
1 Tbsp orange juice
¾ tsp ginger, chopped
¼ orange
orange zest
4 drops sesame oil
1 Tbsp lemon oil
3 Tbsp vegetable oil

PINEAPPLE SHOYU
1 tsp minced garlic
1 tsp minced fresh ginger
⅓ cup brown sugar
⅓ cup pineapple juice
⅓ cup rice vinegar
⅓ cup soy sauce
⅓ cup vegetable stock

FRIED WONTONS
12 wonton wrappers
2 cups vegetable oil

This Pacific Rim-inspired apetizer is always a crowd pleaser it looks complex but is fairly easy to assemble.

Marinade
Combine sweet Thai chili sauce, soy sauce, fresh lime juice, fresh lemon juice, orange juice, chopped ginger and orange zest in a blender and puree until smooth. With the blender still running, slowly drizzle in the sesame oil, lemon oil and vegetable oils.

Pineapple Shoyu
In a sauce pan bring all ingredients (minced garlic, minced fresh ginger, brown sugar, pineapple juice, rice vinegar, soy sauce, vegetable stock) except the slurry to a boil. Reduce the heat and simmer for 15 minutes. Wisk in the corn starch slurry. Bring back to a low boil and cook for three more minutes, stirring frequently to avoid burning.

Wasabi aioli
Combine lemon juice and wasabi powder and wisk until smooth. In a separate bowl stir the sour cream into the mayonnaise and then combine with the wasabi and lemon.

Fried Wontons
Heat 2 cups of vegetable oil in a thick-bottomed, or cast iron, pan on low heat until the temperature reaches 300-325 degrees. Fry wontons until they are light brown. Remove with a slotted spoon and drain onto paper towel.

Tuna and Avocado
Combine tuna, avocado and marinade in a bowl.
Nape (coat with sauce) a 9 inch round plate with 1-2 oz of the shoyu sauce. Place the wasabi aioli in a small squeeze bottle, and squeeze thin paralel lines into the shoyu; use a toothpick to crosshatch the lines. Place one fried wonton in the center of the plate, and place 2 ounces of the tuna on the wonton. Repeat with one more wonton on top of the first.
Garnish the top of the stack with any type of small sprout or micro-green. Drizzle wasabi aioli on top.
Serve with one of the following: Asian slaw with citrus dressing, curly cut cucumber, or pickled ginger. 6 servings.

Black Sesame Sea Scallops

MS | **E**

5 oz sea scallops, per person
2 carrots
1 onion
1 pepper
¼ medium cabbage

WASABI AIOLI
1 cup mayonnaise
¼ cup sour cream
1 Tbsp wasabi powder
1 Tbsp lemon juice

SESAME TUILE DRESSING
¼ cup chopped garlic
¼ cup chopped shallots
¼ cup chopped ginger
½ cup soy sauce
⅛ cup brown sugar
1 cup rice vinegar
1 Tbsp sambal chilie sauce
1 cup cottonseed oil
   ½ cup sesame oil
   ⅛ cup cilantro

TUILE COOKIE
⅜ cup sugar
⅜ cup egg whites,
   at room temperature
½ cup butter
½ cup flour
½ Tbsp sambal chili sauce
½ Tbsp sesame seeds
½ Tbsp lime juice
½ Tbsp almond extract

Julienne cut carrots, onions, peppers, and cabbage.
Season scallops with a pinch of salt and black pepper.
Sear scallops in a hot cast iron skillet or non stick pan, with a small amount of oil, for 3 minutes per side. Don't overcook, so they remain medium inside.
Toss just enough vinaigrette over the vegetables to coat.
Place sauteed vegetables in the center of the plate.
Drizzle a bit more vinaigrette around the plate.
Place scallops on plate.
Drizzle with a little aioli, and place a tuile cookie on top.
Sprinkle with black sesame seeds.

Wasabi Aioli

Mix wasabi powder into the lemon juice.
Add the mayonnaise, and sour
cream, and mix well.

Sesame Tuile Dressing

Blend garlic, shallots, ginger, soy sauce, brown sugar, rice vinegar, and sambal chilie sauce until it is smooth. Slowly add cottonseed oil and sesame oil.
Mix in the chopped cilantro by hand; do not blend.

Tuile Cookie

Mix the sugar and egg whites together.
Melt the butter and fold in the flour. Add in the egg white sugar mixture. Add sambal chili sauce, sesame seeds, lime juice, and almond extract. Keep this batter warm.
On a silpat (silicone baking mat), or parchment lined sheetpan, pipe out or spread a 4 inch long, narrow, thin cookie.
Cook for 10 minutes at 350 degrees.

Crispy Gluten Free Fried Chicken with Apple Jam

6 10 oz airline chicken breast (with wing)
1 qt vegetable oil, as needed

CHICKEN MARINADE
2 cups buttermilk
½ cup gluten-free soy sauce

CHICKEN COATING
1 cup gluten free flour
1½ cup Rice Chex crumbs
1 Tbsp Old Bay seasoning
2 tsp ground black pepper
2 tsp marjoram
½ tsp garlic powder
2 tsp parsley, chopped
½ tsp salt

APPLE JAM
5 Granny Smith apples, peeled,
   cored, and quartered
1 cup yellow onion, diced
1 bay leaf
2 tsp thyme, chopped
¼ tsp ground nutmeg
¼ tsp ground white pepper
1 tsp paprika
⅛ tsp celery seed
1 cup dry white wine
½ cup sugar
2 tsp salt

Marinated Chicken
Combine the soy sauce and the buttermilk, then coat the chicken breasts. Let marinate overnight in the refrigerator.

Chicken Coating/Breading
Put the Rice Chex in a food processor to crumb, then pulse in the gluten free flour, Old Bay seasoning, ground black pepper, marjoram, garlic powder, chopped parsley and salt until evenly mixed.

Pre-heat oil in a home fryer, or a thick bottomed sauce pan, to 350 degrees. Place chicken in pan.
Pre-bake the chicken in a 325 degree oven for 30 to 35 minutes or until an internal temperature of 160 degree is reached. Remove from the oven and let the breasts cool enough so that they can be handled.

Drench each breast in the breading then in buttermilk then back into the breading. Place in the hot oil and fry until they are a light brown turning as needed.
Remove from oil and let drain on a paper towel for a minute.

Apple Jam
Roast apples until soft, 20 to 30 minutes in a 350 degree oven. While the apples are roasting, in a separate pan saute the onion chopped thyme, ground nutmeg, ground white pepper paprika and celery seed, in the oil, when the onions are soft add the wine and salt, simmering to reduce the wine by half. Add the apples and sugar. Cook over a low flame until a jam consistency is achieved. Be sure to use a thick-bottomed sauce pan to avoid burning.

Serving suggestion: mashed potatoes, yams, sautéd kale with shallots garlic.

Tequila Infused Key Lime Pie

MS | D

CRUST
1½ cups graham cracker crumbs
3 Tbsp butter, melted
⅓ cup sugar
1 tsp cinnamon

FILLING
3 cans sweetened condensed milk
½ cup pasteurized egg yolks
¾ cup key lime juice
1 oz tequila
1½ tsp vanilla extract

Crust

Place graham cracker crumbs, melted butter, sugar and cinnamon in a bowl and mix until the butter is completely incorporated into the other ingredients.

Spray a nine-inch spring form pan with pan spray and press the crust mixture into the bottom of the pan.

Make sure the crumbs are spread evenly and firmly compacted. Bake for 4 minutes. Cool.

Filling

Combine egg yolks, vanilla, and condensed milk in a bowl and wisk until smooth.

Wisk in the lime juice and tequila.

Pour into the spring form pan and place in a water bath.

Cook in a 325 degree oven for 20-25 minutes or until firm all the way through.

Cool and remove the spring form ring.

To make a larger and thinner pie use a ten inch pan and reduce the cooking time by 5 minutes.

Serve with lemon gelato, a tuile cookie (recipe on pg 5), and whipped cream.

THE KEY LIME Its exact origins are unknown, but the first formal mention of Key lime pie as a recipe may have been made by William Curry, a ship salvager and Key West's first millionaire; his cook, "Aunt Sally", made the pie for him. If such is the case, however, it is also possible and maybe even probable that Sally adapted the recipe already created by local sponge fishermen. Sponge fishermen spent many contiguous days on their boats, and stored their food on board, including nutritional basics such as canned milk (which would not spoil without refrigeration), limes and eggs. Sponge fishermen at sea would presumably not have access to an oven, and, similarly, the original recipe for Key lime pie did not call for cooking the mixture of lime, milk, and eggs.

BONEYARD SALOON & KITCHEN

Boneyard Saloon & Kitchen is off the beaten path, and that's actually the idea. It's the perfect spot to grab a pint, or meal, with your friends. It's got it all, with six big screens, free and easy parking, and a lovely rooftop bar with sweeping views of the peaks.

On warm summer evenings the large garage door goes up and the cool breeze comes in. Sit at the custom bar, find a community table and make a few friends, or snuggle up in a booth.

Start off with one of the dozens of craft beer selections, or a draft from the Park City Brewing Company, while snacking on gourmet fries. These hand-cut potatoes are sprinkled with truffle oil, parmesan cheese, and parsley, and served in a tower of goodness. They're crispy and delicious.

As an alternative, order the herbed pomme frites, a huge pile of matchstick potatoes served with the same smoked garlic aoli dip. Or nibble on the Amish friendship pretzel, served with sweet country mustard and house-made pickles, or on the pork-belly lettuce wraps.

Then order from the large menu: perhaps something from the custom-built, wood-fired grill. It's the way food has been cooked for centuries, and there's a reason for that. The smoking apple wood adds an aroma and flavor that will make you a believer. So order a half-pound gourmet burger, or baby back ribs with moppin' sauce, or the wood-fired bird sandwich. They're each unique and delicious.

Boneyard Saloon & Kitchen, another Diversified Bars & Restaurants (DBR Inc.) location, ranks as one of the best bars in town, with a Moscow Mule that will kick you back, and a beer menu from around the world that can satisfy even the most discriminating hop head.

Chris Parker has a fine touch with food and the art of food. It's evident as you watch him meticulously prepare items for both Boneyard Saloon & Kitchen, and Wine Dive.

Starting at the age of 15 as a dishwasher, he was soon cooking.

Before coming to Park City, Chris has cooked in New Orleans, in Santa Barbara, California and in Maui where he was Executive Sous Chef under renowned Chef Mark Ellman. Chris also spent two years working under Chef Brent Holleman, who apprenticed under Paul Bocuse, who is considered an ambassodor of modern French Cuisine.

He says, "My style of cooking comes from the experience through my career. Food is my life and wouldn't have it any other way."

Pork Belly Lettuce Wraps

1 pork belly
4 bibb lettuce leaves
2 oz rice noodles
pinch of sesame seeds
2 cups soy sauce
2 cups orange juice
2 cups water,
½ cup brown sugar
1 Tbsp ginger, sliced

2 green onions
2 garlic cloves
1 bay leaf
6 whole peppercorns

SESAME DRESSING
½ cup rice wine vinegar
½ cup soy sauce
1 Tbsp lime juice

1 Tbsp ginger
1 garlic clove
2 Tbsp brown sugar
¼ cup orange juice
1/4 cup sweet Thai chile
1 Tbsp sesame oil
½ cup grapeseed oil

Preheat oven to 350 degrees.
Score pork belly and place in braising pan.
Pour in the soy sauce, orange juice, water, brown sugar, sliced ginger, green onion, garlic, bay leaves, and whole pepper corns. Cover with foil, and braise in oven for 2 ½ hours at 350 degrees. Strain the liquid and save.
Cool overnight in the refrigerator.
Cut into desired portions.
Fry rice noodles at 340 degrees until puffed and crunchy. Drain and set aside.
Toast sesame seeds and set aside.

Dressing
Combine rice wine vinegar, soy sauce, lime juice, ginger, garlic, brown sugar, orange juice, sweet Thai chile and sesame oil into blender.
Add grape seed oil slowly until emulsified.

Assembly
Take reserved liquid, place pork belly in liquid to heat up. If you prefer the dish crispy, cook in oven or deep fry, then put in liquid.
Place bibb lettuce on plate, put belly on lettuce and top with dressing, fried rice noodles, toasted sesame seed.
Serves 4
Enjoy!

RICE NOODLES are a very thin noodle, made of ground rice. They traditionally are not cooked but softened by pouring hot water over them for 10 to 15 minutes. To deep-fry these noodles, use at least 1 1/2 inches of oil. When a noodle is dropped into the oil, puffs up and turns white, the oil is ready. Fry in batches and do not crowd the pan. Remove and let drain on paper towels.

GRAPESEED OIL is a by product of wine making. It has a high smoke point of 421 degrees F, has a light tast and is high in polyunsaturate fats. It is also sprayed on raisins to retain their flavor.

Ahi Burger with Coleslaw

1 big eye tuna belly
1 cup Panko bread crumbs
6 lettuce leaves
1 tomato, sliced
¼ head cabbage
1 carrot
1 shallot
1 jalapeno
1 green onion
Tbsp parsley
1 lemon, juiced

6 brioche buns
salt and pepper to taste

PICO DE GALLO
1 tomato
¼ cup red onions
½ cup cilantro
1 lime juice, juiced
1 jalapeno

TOMATILLO VERDE SALSA
5 tomatillos, grilled
2 jalapenos
1 lime, juiced
water
salt and pepper to taste

SAMBAL OLEK AIOLI
1 Tbsp mayonnaise
1 Tbsp sambal
1 Tbsp lime Juice
salt and pepper to taste

Freeze tuna before grinding tuna into bowl.
In a Cuisinart grind the tuna, and place into into a large bowl. Sset aside.
Finely chop carrot, celery, shallot, jalapeno, green onion, parsley. Add Panko bread crumbs and chopped vegetables to ground tuna and mix well.
Form mixture into 5-ounce tuna patties.

Pico de Gallo
Chop and combine tomatoes, red onions, cilantro, lime juice and jalapenos.

Tomatillo Verde Salsa
Puree grilled tomatillos, jalapenos, water, salt and pepper.

Sambal Olek Aioli
Mix together mayonnaise, sambal, lime juice, salt and pepper.

Coleslaw
Shred the cabbage into a large bowl. Add pico de gallo and verde salsa. Mix well.

Sear Ahi burger on flat top or saute pan each side for 4 minutes or till cooked through.
Toast the bun, and top with sambal aioli, coleslaw, tuna patty, lettuce leafe and a slice of tomato.
Serve with home fries (we mix ours with White truffle oil, Asiago cheese and parsley). Add lemon wedge.
Add lemon wedge and enjoy!

Serves 6

Baby Back Ribs with Moppin' Sauce

PORK AND PORK DRY RUB
1 pork baby back rib rack
¼ cup chili powder
¼ cup cumin
2 Tbsp coriander
2 Tbsp garlic powder
2 Tbsp onion powder
2 tsp cayenne pepper
2 Tbsp kosher salt
½ cup brown sugar

ROOT BEER BAR-B-Q
2 cans root beer
1 yellow onion
1 Tbsp garlic, chopped
1 bay leaf
1 Tbsp whole black peppercorns
4 cups ketchup
¼ cup worcestershire
½ cup red wine vinegar
½ cup brown sugar
½ cup soy sauce

CORN BREAD MUFFINS
1 ¼ cup all purpose flour
⅔ cup cornmeal
⅓ cup sugar
1 Tbsp baking powder
½ tsp salt
2 cups milk
½ cup canola oil.

COLESLAW DRESSING
3 cups mayo
1 Tbsp celery seed
1 cup white wine vinegar
1 ½ cup sugar

Preheat over to 425 degrees.
Dry rub ribs with chili powder, cumin, coriander, garlic powder, onion powder, cayenne pepper, kosher salt, and the brown sugar.
Let marinate over night in the refrigerator.
Sear the ribs on the grill for 3 minutes on each side, to seal in flavor.
Place in a roasting pan and cover with ⅓ of the Moppin' sauce, and ⅓ water. Cover and braise for 3½ hours at 425 degrees.

Moppin' Sauce
Saute yellow onions, garlic, bay leaf and black pepper corns until translucent.
Add the root beer and slow boil to reduce by a third of volume. Add ketchup, Worcestershire, red wine vinegar, brown sugar and Soy sauce continue to reduce on medium heat by another one third of volume.

Corn Bread Muffins
Preheat overn to 400 degrees.
Mix together flour, cornmeal, sugar, baking powder, and salt. Add milk and canola oil and mix well. Bake at 400 degrees for 30 min.

Coleslaw Dressing
Mix together mayo, celery seed, white wine vinegar, and sugar.

ColeSlaw
Slice green cabbage and mix with dressing

Serve ribs with cornbread muffins
and house made coleslaw.

Serves 2

BUTCHER'S CHOP HOUSE & BAR

OM

This contemporary steakhouse, by Diversified Bars & Restaurants (DBR Inc), has something for the entire family. Steaks, chops, seafood, pasta, salads, and more. All of this in Butcher's beautifully finished cherry wood dining room and bar, with one of the finest wine lists and back bar liquor displays in Utah. Take in spectacular mountain views while you dine in the center of Park City's action at the base of the Town Lift.

To quickly quell your hunger, start out with some bleu cheese stuffed dates, polenta crusted fried calamari, or an Ahi tuna poke, served in lettuce cups with onions, sesame seeds, and Sriracha. For an entree go wild on the Filet Oscar, with its topping of dungeness crab, or pasta Bolognese in Butcher's signature buffalo meat sauce, or an Ahi filet with Szechuan stir-fried vegetables. They're all beautifully presented and delicious.

Of course there's meat for every appetite. Butcher's steaks are legendary. They're all hand-cut, and certified Angus Beef using only sustainable ranching practices, from the 8-ounce Filet Mignon to the 24-ounce Porterhouse. Or there's the Bone-in Ribeye, New York Steak or Prime Rib. Hungry for a pork chop? Then order the Niman Ranch thick cut 12-ounce chop. For a taste of down under, order the New Zealand lamb rib chops. Even the side dishes are savory, such as the Jalapeno Mac n Cheese, or the Coconut Jasmine rice. You might want to add a half-pound of King crab legs to your order just for the heck of it.

A "must eat" restaurant while you're in town, Butcher's is "elegance without arrogance," as the motto says. It's comfortable, delicious, and the perfect place to finish your perfect day in Park City.

Jose Cuellar's eyes sparkle as he talks of what he likes to cook. "I really like the winter mushroom buffalo, with huckleberry glaze," he says, "and, really, all of the wild game. I like to experiment."

After working with a variety of "schooled chefs", the realization of Jose's "real world" experiences put him into his executive role. His passion and attention to detail are demonstrated by the superb quality of his cuisine.

Chef Cuellar has been the head chef at Butcher's Chop House and Bar as well as at No Name Saloon and Grill for the past 6 years, but has been working at Butcher's since they opened 12 years ago. Butcher's is a big-city chop house, situated nicely in the middle of Park City's famous mountains. As a local son, Jose is doing exactly what he wants to do, where he wants to do it.

PG20 PG21 PG22

Buffalo Pasta Bolognese

1 lb penne pasta
2 lbs buffalo meat, ground
2 carrots, diced
1 yellow onion, diced
4 celery stalks, diced
2 fresh garlic cloves

3 Tbsp fresh parsley, chopped
3 cups red wine
8 oz can of tomato sauce
salt & pepper to taste
2 Tbsp olive oil

In a large pot bring penne pasta to a boil and cook pasta *al dente*. In separate skillet, heat olive oil over medium heat. Add onions, celery and carrots and cook gently to sweat for about 2 minutes. Add garlic and cook for an additional minute.

Add buffalo meat and salt and pepper and brown meat. To keep meat from clumping together make sure to chop as it cooks.

Simmer over medium heat, add red wine and reduce by 50%. Add tomato sauce and parsley and bring all ingredients to a boil.

Stir in pasta and serve.

Pan Seared Mahi Mahi with Risotto

2 8 oz. mahi mahi filets	RISOTTO	ROASTED RED PEPPER VINAIGRETTE
2 cups Panko bread crumbs	8 oz arborio rice, uncooked	1 can roasted red peppers
3 Tbsp fresh parsley	½ lb butter	1 yellow onion, diced
2 Tbsp fresh rosemary	6 cups chicken stock	2 garlic cloves, diced
1 cup buttermilk	1 cup white table wine	1 cup white table wine
salt & pepper to taste	1 pinch saffron	1 cup balsamic vinegar
		salt & pepper to taste

Mahi Mahi

In a large mixing bowl, place the mahi mahi filets. Pour the buttermilk over the filets and let them soak. In a separate bowl, mix bread crumbs with parsley, rosemary and salt & pepper. Remove buttermilk filets and, one by one, coat filets in Panko/herb crust mixture. Place breaded filets in skillet and pan-sear in canola oil until cooked through.

Risotto

In a large skillet melt butter and brown the arborio rice. Add white wine and reduce by half.
Over low heat add chicken stock and reduce again by half, then mix in saffron, cook for 8-10 minutes.

Vinaigrette

In a medium skillet, sauté roasted red peppers, onion, garlic, salt & pepper until onions are soft. Over medium heat add white wine and balsamic vinegar and bring to boil. Reduce mixture by 25 percent then while hot, pour vinaigrette sauce into food processor and blend for 2 minutes..

On a platter, place mahi mahi on bed of cooked risotto.
Spoon roasted red pepper vinaigrette over filets and serve.

Filet Oscar

2 6 oz filets
salt & pepper rub
2 oz lump crab meat
butter

BÉARNAISE SAUCE
6 egg yolks
½ cup white table wine
½ cup belted butter (unsalted)
1 tsp Tabasco® sauce

2 Tbls lemon juice
3 sprigs fresh tarragon
salt & pepper to taste

Rub filets in salt and pepper rub. Cook filets to desired temperature, (suggested temp - medium rare) Note: char broil steaks do not continuously turn steaks when cooking .
In small sauté pan, melt butter to coat pan and sauté lump crab.

Béarnaise Sauce

In a steel bowl, whip egg yolks and wine together over a pan of boiling water until thickened. Remove from heat. Slowly whip butter adding the rest the Tabasco®, lemon juice, fresh tarragon and salt and pepper to taste.
Place finished steak on platter top with sautéed crab and spoon béarnaise sauce over top.
Serves 3-4

At Butchers we use the filet cut because it is the tradition on this particular dish, but feel free to use any cut of beef that you prefer.
Served with mashed potatoes and asparagus.

Serves 3-4

DEER VALLEY
GROCERY~CAFÉ

DEER VALLEY GROCERY - CAFÉ

DV

Enjoy the view and mountain air while dining lakeside on the outdoor deck at Deer Valley Grocery~Café.

Open for breakfast, lunch and early supper, the Café serves fresh roasted coffee and espresso drinks, and a seasonal menu featuring salads made with local ingredients, panini sandwiches, creative appetizer and entrée specials, freshly baked breads, desserts, cakes and other items. The Deer Valley Grocery~Café has a selection of gourmet grocery items, house-prepared take-away entrees, as well as wine, beer and liquor.

The dishes featured in this cookbook reflect the tastes of the summer of 2015. The house-favorite fish tacos change seasonally. The version here was inspired by fresh citrus, char flavor from the grill and finishing with a little crunch. The avocado beet toast was born out of our love of hummus, but we wanted to put a new spin on it. This hummus is almost an equal mix of beets and chickpeas, so you get that traditional hummus flavor, but with a bright beet twist.

At the Deer Valley Grocery~Café we like to use sustainable fish and local ingredients whenever possible. Featured in the following recipes are Copper Moose Farms produce and locally sourced fish, tomatoes and basil. Many of our dishes can be made to order gluten-free or vegan, which many of our customers like.

Chef Kristine Thorslund finds inspiration in many places when creating recipes: seasonality of ingredients, recipes she's come across and remembered from the past, travels, and the dishes she learned from her mother and grandmother.

Deer Valley Grocery–Cafe Chef Kristine Thorslund, is a 14-year employee of Deer Valley Resort. She has served as the Deer Valley Grocery~Café chef since May 2013.

Kristine started at the resort as a culinary intern from the Culinary Institute of America in Hyde Park, New York. After a successful internship she returned to Deer Valley as the assistant Royal Street Café sous chef.

Kristine spent three years fine-tuning her skills at the famous Fireside Dining during the winter, and assisting with the resort's many banquet operations during the summer season. Before becoming the Deer Valley Grocery~Café's chef, Kristine also served as the assistant sous chef at Empire Canyon Lodge.

Kristine is originally from Seattle, Wasington and currently resides in the small town of Francis, Utah, with her husband, David Knose, and their daughter, Emma. She enjoys swimming, skiing, camping, spending time with her family and traveling.

Avocado Beet Toast

6 slices Deer Valley Wild Rice Harvest bread, thinly sliced and toasted (or substitute your favorite grain bread)
3 avocados thinly sliced, half per toast
6 oz Shephard Dairy goat cheese, crumbled, 1oz per toast
6 tsp lemon mosto oil, 1 tsp per toast
Hawaiian black sea salt, to taste

black pepper to taste
1½ cups micro greens ¼ cup per toast
3 tsp butter; ½ tsp per toast

BEET HUMMUS
1 15 oz can Garbanzo beans
¼ cup tahini
2 medium to large beets

1 lemon
1 orange
2 Tbsp mint
2 Tbsp dill
2 garlic cloves
¼ cup olive oil
Salt and pepper to taste

Toast bread and spread with butter.
Peel and cut avocados into thin slices.
Spread each slice of toast with ¼ cup beet hummus.
Place half of a sliced avocado over hummus.
Top with crumbled goat cheese and micro greens. Sprinkle with black sea salt and pepper to taste. Finish with lemon oil.

Beet Hummus
Steam or boil one of the beets, let chill, then peel and roughly chop.
Peel and chop remaining raw beet.
Drain and rinse garbanzo beans.
Add beets to a food processor, and process until smooth.
Add garbanzo beans, tahini, lemon juice, orange juice, mint, dill, garlic and olive oil, process again until smooth.
Season with salt and pepper to taste. Chill until needed.

Serves 6

Deer Valley Grocery Cafe Caprese Salad

1 16 oz tub pearl mozzarella
1 ½ cups olive oil
1 lemon zested
4 rosemary sprigs, whole
4 medium to large heirloom tomatoes
8 oz cherry tomatoes or baby heirlooms
4 Tbsp lemon mosto oil

edible flower petals
1 bunch basil, chiffonade
salt and pepper, to taste

BLACKBERRY BALSAMIC TAR
2 pints black berries
2 pints balsamic vinegar (good quality!)

BALSAMIC PEARLS*
7oz balsamic vinegar
1/3 tsp agar agar
1 cup olive oil

*Balsamic pearls are available online too)

Drain pearl mozzarella.
Marinate in ½ cup olive oil, rosemary and lemon zest.
Cut large heirloom tomatoes into wedges and cherry tomatoes in half (or quarters if large).
Cut basil into long thin strips (chiffonade).

Assembly
Coat a portion of plate or platter with blackberry balsamic tar (use ¾ - ½ the plate for a dramatic presentation).
Arrange tomato wedges, cherry tomatoes and pearl mozzarella on balsamic tar.
Season with salt and pepper, to taste.
Top with basil chiffonade, flower petals, lemon mosto oil and balsamic pearls.

Blackberry Balsamic Tar
Combine black berries and balsamic vinegar and reduce over low heat until a syrup consistency is achieved.
Note: The better the balsamic the better the syrup!

Balsamic Pearls
Place olive oil in a tall glass in the freezer for at least 30 minutes. (It's better if you use a tall glass so that there is more time for the balsamic vinegar droplets to get cold and gel before reaching the bottom.)
Once the oil has been in the freezer for at least 30 minutes, put the balsamic vinegar in a saucepan and dissolve in the agar agar.
Bring to a boil, stirring constantly with a beater. Take off of the heat and skim to eliminate any impurities.

Serves 4-6

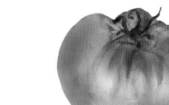

BALSAMIC PEARLS *The cold oil spherification method consists of cooling droplets of a hot agar solution 35° C (95° F) and releasing them in cold oil using a syringe or pipette (or a squirt bottle with a fine opening). Agar must to be heated to boil for jelling and sets at a temperature of about 35 - 45° C (95° - 113° F). The droplets must to cool down and set before they reach the* bottom of the cold oil container to keep a nice spherical shape.

AGAR AGAR *produced from a variety of seaweeds, is a thickener and stabilizer. Agar agar is used in many dairy-free, vegan, and vegetarian dishes. It is used in custards, puddings and sauces.*

Fish Tacos

1½ lbs salmon cut into 12 pieces, 2 per taco
24 6 inch white corn tortillas - 2 per taco
12 scallions, grilled
2 limes, cut into wedges
1½ cups pumpkin seeds, toasted
3 Tbsp olive oil
1 poblano pepper
salt and pepper to taste
6 cups shredded cabbage
   (purple, green or mix)

6 cups oil (canola-olive oil blend or
   vegetable oil)

ROASTED POBLANO GUACAMOLE
4 ripe avocados
1 grilled poblano pepper (from above)
2 limes
2 garlic cloves
salt and pepper to taste
1 Tbsp olive oil

SLAW DRESSING
1½ cups mayo
1 lemon juiced and zest
1 lime juiced and zested
1 orange juiced and zested
salt and pepper to taste

FISH DUST
1 cup rice flour
½ cup Deer Valley Oomph!!
1 Tbsp salt

Turn grill on, and heat frying oil to 350° F and oven to 350 degrees.

Coat pumpkin seeds with 2tbs olive oil and salt and pepper. Toast in oven for 5 minutes or until golden brown. Cool and roughly chop, set aside.

Cut salmon into 1 in strips or 12 long pieces (depending on the width of fish).

Coat in Fish Dust, see recipe below.

Coat scallions with 1 tablespoon of olive oil.

Grill until soft and bright green. Cut into 2 in pieces, set aside.

Coat poblano peppers with olive oil.

Grill until black. Place in a bowl and cover with plastic wrap, wait 5 minutes. Then remove blacked skin and seeds.

Fish Dust

Mix all rice flour, Deer Valley Oomph!!, and salt together.
Set aside until needed.

Slaw dressing

Zest and juice the lemon, lime and orange, combine in a bowl. Mix with mayonnaise and salt and pepper to taste.

Roasted Poblano Guacamole

Peel and pit the avocados. Place avocados, juice from limes, garlic and olive oil in a food processor and process until smooth. Season with salt and pepper to taste. Fold in the poblano peppers.

Assembly

Coat salmon with fish dust and fry in batches for 3 minutes, or until fish is firm.

Mix shredded cabbage with slaw dressing.

Heat tortillas on the grill until warm.

Use two tortillas per taco. Place dressed cabbage, grilled scallions and salmon on tortillas. Top with guacamole and chopped pumpkin seeds, serve with a lime wedge.

Serves 4-6 people, makes 12 tacos.

DONE TO YOUR TASTE
CATERING & EVENTS

DONE TO YOUR TASTE
CATERING & EVENTS

DONE TO YOUR TASTE

K

DALTON CAMPBELL

Since 1995, Done To Your Taste Catering and Events has earned an impeccable reputation for preparing fresh, regional cuisine and creative presentations.

Proprietor Eileen Dunn honed her culinary skills in the early 1980's, working in Deer Valley's world-class kitchens. She then worked at Park City's original Barking Frog and Riverhorse restaurants under Chef David Harries.

Today, Done To Your Taste is renowned for mouth-watering specialties infused with nature's finest and freshest ingredients, which promise to delight even the most discerning palette. Presenting a full range of catering and event services, Done To Your Taste has been widely recognized for its culinary standards in a town that caters to world-class customers.

Done To Your Taste partners with local farmers and ranchers for exceptional quality meats, while growing herbs and vegetables in its Kamas Valley gardens. Freshness is guaranteed, no matter the season, with specialties ranging from Eileen's famous housemade chips and salsas to signature barbecue, seasonal cocktails and elaborate fare.

Events are expertly executed by an experienced staff of planners, decorators, chefs, bartenders and servers.

Done To your Taste has a colorful list of preferred locations, including Sundance venues, art galleries, ranches, gardens and social halls, and specializes in private chef and catering services in your home as well. Whether black tie or black fleece, DTYT promises to transform any setting into a sumptuous affair. For a seamless event that makes a lasting impression, count on Done To Your Taste Catering and Events.

Chef Dalton Campbell has a burning passion for food. He began his career in the culinary field at the age of thirteen, though he began cooking as soon as he was tall enough to stand on a step stool and reach the stove.

He comes from a culinarily talented family, and though he has not had any formal training he has developed a unique gourmet cooking style of his own.

Finally Dalton took over the Executive Chef position at Done To your Taste Catering. Over the years he has developed a unique, simple, fresh, culinary style incorporating the techniques of authentic Mexican, Mediterranean, Italian, French, and Asian cuisines, as well as their artistic presentations. He has created a diverse, New American cuisine of his own cooking purely from passion and soul.

PG36   PG37   PG38   PG39   PG40

Grilled Firecracker Shrimp Skewers

32 26-30 count/lb raw tiger shrimp
3-4 links andouille sausage, fully cooked
16 8 inch bamboo skewers
3 Tbsp sambal chili paste
1½ Tbsp minced garlic
3 Tbsp olive oil

2 Tbsp fresh lime juice
1 tsp sesame oil
1 tsp kosher salt
½ tsp cracked black pepper
2 tsp smoked paprika
chopped cilantro and lime wedges for garnish

For an incredible surf and turf dinner try our firecracker shrimp with our chimichurri flank steak; they pair very well together.

Substitute larger 16-20 count/lb shrimp to bulk up the protein for a full entrée portion.

Peel and devein shrimp, pat dry and then set them aside in a small bowl.

In a separate small bowl combine sambal chili paste, minced garlic, olive oil, lime juice, sesame oil, salt, pepper, and smoked paprika.

Stir to combine and cover shrimp in the marinade.

Let marinate for at least 2 hours in the fridge.

Soak the bamboo skewers in water (to prevent burning).

Preheat grill to medium high heat.

Slice andouille sausage into 16 ½ inch medallions.

Skewer 2 shrimp per skewer with 1 piece of sausage in the middle.

Grill for approximately 2 minutes per side then transfer to a serving plate.

Garnish with chopped cilantro and lime wedges.

Serve immediately.

Serves 8

Golden Beet and Fennel Slaw
with White Balsamic Dijon Vinaigrette

SLAW
4 cups green cabbage thinly sliced
1 cup red cabbage thinly sliced
2 cups julienned golden beets
1 cup julienned carrots
1 large red bell pepper julienned
½ bulb fennel thinly sliced

VINAIGRETTE
1 Tbsp whole grain dijon mustard
1 Tbsp honey
1 lemon, juiced
4 Tbsp white balsamic vinegar
5 Tbsp olive oil
½ tsp kosher salt

This recipe makes a perfect, out of the ordinary, salad for a summer BBQ or picnic lunch; it will surely leave your guests impressed. If possible try to find the produce for this recipe at your local farmers market in late summer when golden beets, heirloom carrots, fennel and cabbage are in the peak of their growing season; the fresh produce will speak for itself.

Vinaigrette
In the blender start with the white balsamic vinegar, lemon juice, honey, salt, and Dijon mustard. Turn on low speed and slowly drizzle in the olive oil to emulsify the vinaigrette.

Slaw
Thinly slice the green and red cabbage and fennel.
Peel and julienne the golden beets and carrots.
Julienne the red pepper. Mix all vegetables in a medium bowl and toss with the vinaigrette.

Serves 8

Chimichurri Flank Steak

STEAK
1-2 flank steaks, approximately 4 lbs
2 Tbsp freshly minced garlic
2 tsp ground cumin
2 tsp chili powder
1 tsp onion powder
2 tsp dry oregano
2 tsp kosher salt
1 tsp cracked pepper

1 lemon, juiced
2 Tbsp olive oil

CHIMICHURRI
2 cups cilantro
2 cups flat leaf Italian parsley
5 garlic cloves
⅓ cup red wine vinegar
½ cup olive oil

3 Tbsp fresh lemon juice
½ tsp oregano
1 tsp fresh thyme
1 tsp cumin
½ tsp kosher salt
½ tsp cracked black pepper
1 tsp red pepper flakes

The chimichurri flank steak is a perfect entrée for a hot summer day. The South American chimichurri makes a beautiful refreshing accompaniment that brightens up the steak, giving it a fresh summer flare just as if you were sitting on the coastline in Argentina. Enjoy with a frozen margarita, or a light Mexican beer with a fresh wedge of lime, such as a Modelo Especial or a Pacifico.

Steak
Prepare a spice rub with cumin, chili powder, oregano, onion powder, salt, and pepper.
Drizzle the flank steak with olive oil and rub with fresh garlic, and liberally season both sides of steak with spice rub.
Place in a gallon bag along with the juice of one lemon, in the fridge and marinate at least 4 hours or overnight.
Remove and let sit for 45 minutes at room temperature.
Preheat grill to medium high heat and grill the steak for approx. 5 minutes per side to medium rare, adjusting time depending on thickness. Give the steak a quarter turn half way through grilling on each side; this will allow the steak to cook evenly and will also create beautiful grill marks.
Place on a cutting board and let the steak rest for at least 5 minutes before slicing. Slice in thin 2-3 inch strips across the grain, drizzle with chimichurri and enjoy.

Chimichurri
Put cilantro, parsley, garlic cloves, red wine vinegar, lemon juice, thyme, oregano, cumin, salt, pepper, and red pepper flake in a blender at low speed, and slowly drizzle in the olive oil.

Makes 8 Servings

Harvest Barley Risotto with Sweet Corn Succotash

RISOTTO
2 cups pearl barley
2 Tbsp butter
¾ cup shredded parmesan cheese
2 cup white wine, chardonnay
2 cup half and half
2 cup chicken or vegetable stock
1 medium yellow onion
1 Tbsp minced garlic

1 tsp truffle oil
2½ tsp kosher salt
1 tsp cracked black pepper

SLURRY
1 Tbsp corn starch
2 Tbsp cold water

SWEET CORN SUCCOTASH
2 ears fresh sweet corn
1 medium yellow onion
1 Tbsp minced garlic
1 pint heirloom cherry tomatoes
2 medium-small Zucchini
2 cups purple kale
2 Tbsp butter
salt and pepper to taste

Risotto

Boil barley in salted water until tender, about 45 minutes.
Cut the yellow onion into a small dice and sauté in a medium sauce pan with butter.
Once caramelized, add the minced garlic and sauté for another 4 minutes, then add the white wine.
Bring to a simmer and reduce until there are only a few tablespoons of wine left.
Add chicken stock and half and half, and bring to a simmer.
Drain the barley once it has finished cooking and add to the sauce pan.
Bring to a simmer and mix in parmesan cheese and corn starch and water mixture (slurry). Add salt, pepper, and truffle oil and enjoy alongside the sweet corn succotash.

Succotash

Cut the yellow onion into a small dice and sauté in a medium skillet with butter until lightly caramelized.
Cut corn kernels off the ears of corn, dice the zucchini, cut cherry tomatoes in half, and chop the kale.
Once the onions are caramelized add minced garlic, corn, and zucchini and sauté 5 minutes or until zucchini starts to brown.
Add the cherry tomatoes and kale.
Sauté for another 3 minutes or until the kale is tender. Salt and pepper to taste and enjoy with harvest risotto.
Enjoy with a nice glass of Sauvignon Blanc.

Grilled Peach and Black Plum Skewers with Lavender Honey and Almond Chantilly Cream

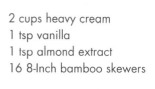

4 ripe fresh peaches
5 ripe fresh black plums
1 Tbsp olive oil
3 Tbsp lavender honey*

2 cups heavy cream
1 tsp vanilla
1 tsp almond extract
16 8-Inch bamboo skewers

This light refreshing summer dessert pairs beautifully with a nice Moscato. To kick the presentation up a notch, replace the bamboo skewers with thick lavender sprigs, leaving the lavender flower buds on the tip of the sprig and stripping off the rest. Skewer peaches and plums on the lavender sprig starting at the base.

When grilling keep the flower portion off the edge of the grill.

Almond Chantilly Cream

Start with a chilled bowl using either a stand up kitchen mixer with a whisk attachment, or a hand mixer, and whip the heavy cream until soft peaks form.

Add half of lavender honey (1½ Tbsp), vanilla, and almond extract, and whip to incorporate.

Cover and set aside in fridge until ready to serve.

Assembly

Soak the bamboo skewers in water to prevent them from burning while on the grill.

Preheat your grill to a medium heat.

Slice the fresh peaches and plums into ½ inch segments and lightly brush them with olive oil.

Skewer the peaches and plums alternating every other segment.

Grill the skewers approximately 2 minutes per side until well caramelized.

Drizzle with 1.5 Tbsp of the lavender honey and serve immediately with the almond chantilly cream.

Serves 8

*If you cannot find lavender honey you can add 2 drops of food grade essential lavender oil into 3 t of regular honey.

SAMPSON
COMSTOCK
RED FOX
HAWK EYE
10TH MOUNTAIN

FLANAGAN'S ON MAIN

FATHER FLANAGAN

If you're looking for authenticity on Main Street, then head in to Flanagan's on Main. This is a cozy, raucous pub with good grub, live music, and fun times. For the past 7 years they have been serving "pub grub on steroids," according to Tommy Bergin, general manager, in a 120-year-old building that once housed a candy store, and Chinese restaurant among other things.

It's family friendly, with a full liquor license, with support from local purveyors Park City and Epic Brewing, as well as Jameson's Irish Whiskey and Guinness Stout. Dine in the cozy alcove and watch the scene on Main Street, or belly up to the bar for a bite and a pint of one of their 12 beers on tap, or one of the 20 bottled beers.

Downstairs is the scene for evening action. "It's the ultimate man cave," says Bergin. There are 11 television screens so you can watch the game, all while cozying up on the couch. It's also an intimate music venue where artists such as Jon Bon Jovi and Richie Sambora have performed, as well as local acts. Tuesday night is Trivia Night, or you can challenge your friends to a board game. Wing Wednesday offers $.60 wings, with their 911 sauce if you dare. Thirsty Thursdays means $3 PBRs or $5 local draft beers.

From the kitchen, start with the Dubliner hot wings, Ahi crostini, or corned beef sliders. The authentic fish and chips is their most popular item, followed closely by the Irish Stew, which has been slow cooked in Guinness Stout. Savor the Chicken Boxty, stewed with onions, mushrooms, and garlic in an Irish whiskey cream sauce, while downing a pint of draft. Flanagan's recently won the prestigious "Perfect Pint Award" in Los Angeles for the way they pour their Guinness, with its creamy head. It's all about brews, blues, and stews.

In the early 1900's, Father E.J. Flanagan, with the help of the Union Pacific Railroad, founded an orphanage in Nebraska which would later be known worldwide as Boys Town.

Flanagan, accompanied by a young orphan named Charlie Kenworthy, stopped annually in Park City to raise funds for his charitable endeavor. In a pavilion directly across from Flanagan's on Main, the event included a 2-hour minstrel show, finishing with Charlie's plea: "I come to you as a salesman for I have something to sell. I am dealing in human hearts, in love. The love of a homeless waif is for sale and it is my business to sell it to you." And the silver miners, millionaires, and ladies of the night responded more than generously.

PG46 PG47 PG48 PG49 PG50

Flanagan's Blackend Ahi Crostini

4 oz ahi tuna, per serving
Chef Paul Prudhomme's Magic Bend Seasoning
1 ciabatta bread roll
1 med sized avocado
1 lime, cut into wedges
sriracha, drizzle to taste preference

CILANTRO PEPITA DRESSING
1 bunch cilantro (leaves only)
¼ cup pepita*
1 Tbsp Dijon mustard
2 cloves garlic
1 lime juiced
¼ cup of rice wine vinegar
¾ Tbsp kosher salt
¾ tsp course black pepper
1 cup canola oil

PICO DE GALLO
6 plum tomatoes
½ onion
1 bunch cilantro
1 lime, juice
½ lemon, juiced
1 red bell pepper

Coat fish in Chef Paul Prudhomme's Magic Bend Seasoning
In a hot skillet place ahi searing each side for only 10 seconds then let stand and cool. When cooled slice into 4 1oz pieces.
Cut ciabatta in 4 slices. Toast.
Peel and pit avocado and cut into 4 pieces.
Place on plate then put one tablespoon of cilantro pepita, ¼ avocado, Pico de Gallo, a drizzle of sriracha sauce and a squeeze of lime.
Garnish with lime wedges.

Cilantro Pepita Dressing

Into a mixer combine cilantro, leaves only, pepita, Dijon mustard, garlic, lime juice, rice wine vinegar, kosher salt and black pepper.
Add oil slowly while mixer is still running and blend till smooth.

Pico de Gallo

Clean the inside of tomatoes then dice.
Dice onion, red pepper, cilantro
Place tomatoes, onions, cilantro, lime, and red pepper in a mixing bowl.
Squeeze in juice of lime and lemon.
Spoon mix all ingredients

BLACKENED AHI CROSTINI "Not exactly a traditional Irish dish, but what flavors! The sriracha controls the heat, the lime juice adds a cooling agent. And with our house made Pico de Gallo it is a customer and staff favorite. In fact this is Flanagans this is our best seller. Being surrounded by some of the best restaurants in the country, we are not typical 'Pub Grub' and have risen to the occassion."

— Tommy, executive chef, Flanagan's

*PEPITAS Pumpkin seeds.

Potato Leek Soup

6 cups leeks, sliced, white and light
    green parts only
4 cups onions, diced
4 cups celery, chopped
6 medium russet potatoes
    (3 ½ - 4 lbs) peeled, coarsely chopped

1 cup hot water
4 cups heavy cream
¼ cup canola oil

In an large stock pot, over high heat, add canola oil and sauté onions, celery and ½ of the leeks until vegetables are soft.
Add water and bring to a boil.
Roughly chop the potatoes and add to the leeks. Simmer for approximately 45 minutes.
Add heavy cream and return to a boil for 15 minutes. Add in the rest of the leeks and remove from heat. Add salt and pepper to taste.

Serves 6

"POTATO LEEK SOUP is an old family recipe which, over the years we touched up a little, but always kept with the with the old school philosophy of a great tasting soup with great texture to warm your heart on a cold day. Having the leeks split into two different cooking times gives more flavors and different textures to every spoon full. We make it fresh every day and in winter time twice a day. A Flanagan's staple which you can order by the bowl, cup, or side dish."
— *Tommy, executive chef, Flanagan's*

Whiskey Chicken Boxty

8 oz chicken breast per serving, cubed
½ cup mushrooms, sliced
1 cup heavy cream
1 tsp chopped thyme
2 Tbsp butter, rolled in flour
2 oz Jameson Irish Whiskey
1 tsp chopped garlic
¼ cup canola oil

BOXTY
8 oz dried potatoes
4 medium russet potatoes
3 qts cold water
1 ½ qts milk
8 cups white flour
5-6 eggs
salt- to taste

Heat canola oil in a medium sauté pan over medium/high heat. When oil is hot add chicken and sauté approximately 3 minutes a side season with salt and pepper. Add garlic, mushrooms, and thyme and sauté quickly, then add in half of the whiskey. After alcohol has burned off, add heavy cream and butter,(roll butter in flour to help thicken sauce). Before serving add other half of whiskey and let alcohol burn off.
To serve: Place ⅓ sauce on bottom of plate, add boxty, place ½ chicken on to top of boxty, fold boxty over and put remainder of sauce and chicken on top.

Boxty

In a mixer combine dried potatoes, milk, and water, Mix on low speed adding flour 4 cups at a time till thoroughly mixed.

In a separate bowl beat the eggs, add in beaten eggs to the dried potato flour mixture and continue to mix.
Peel and grate the raw potatoes and add to mix. Mix well. Use 8 oz. ladle and cook boxty as you would a crape or pancake on a griddle till golden brown.
Serves 6

BOXTY *"A filler for most Irish moms. It is used when you had a family of 6 but only enough food for 4. It is a filler that helps spread the meal out so everyone was full. When mom didn't have enough money for bread and a backyard full of potatoes, she would grab some potatoes, boil them up, smash them and mix with milk or water till it was like a pancake batter. By using a ladle she was able to scoop out and and place on a griddle or large pan to make a Boxty. A Boxty can be used in Sheppard's Pie, Irish Stew, Corn beef and cabbage, or any dish you wish to put a little Irish history."*

WHISKEY CHICKEN BOXTY *"A good friend taught me this dish using a traditional Irish Boxty, and combining a flair with chicken, garlic, scallions, heavy cream, and of course Irish whiskey!! As I tell all my customers, 'you can never go wrong combining heavy cream and Irish whiskey'. Our whiskey of choice is Jameson Irish Whiskey."*

— *Tommy, executive chef, Flanagan's*

Irish Beef Stew

10 cups cubed stew meat
6 cups Guinness Stout
4 cups onions

¼ canola oil
4 cups celery
4 cups carrots

3 cups water
⅛ cup beef base
2 cups flour

In a large stockpot, brown cubed beef for approximately 10 minutes making sure beef is browned on all sides.
Add in onions, celery, carrots, and sauté until onions are soft.
Add in flour and mix well.
Once flour is mixed in, add the water and beef base stirring in water and simmer.
Add Guinness and bring stew to a simmer.
Let simmer for approximately 3 hours.
Serve with mashed potatoes and toasted bread.

Serves 6

IRISH BEEF STEW "*My mother use to say, 'The best part of making a stew or anything in a crock pot is putting it together setting it on low temp. and then you have the next 3 to 4 hours to get errands done, clean the house,or fold the laundry.' This is very impotant in any busy house. You can make it the day of or a day before. All the flavors soak into the meats and gravy. We took a basic Irish stew recipe and with the addition of Guinness made an Irish stew that sticks to your ribs with goodness. I prefer ciabatta bread as my toast, but whatever toast you use to dip into your gravy works. The flour thickens your gravy and the mashed potato puts it all together. Some advice on the cubed beef is to not overcook it, medium rare at most, it will be soaking in flavor and cooking throughout stewing time.*"
— Tommy, executive chef, Flanagan's

"Sheppard's" Pie

MS | **E**

2 lbs ground beef
½ lb ground lamb
3 cups onions, diced
1½ cups peas
1½ cups carrots
3 Tbsp Bisto Gravy Powder
1½ Tbsp beef base
5 cups hot water

5 Tbsp Worcestershire sauce
5 Tbsp Worcestershire sauce
6 Tbsp tomato paste
1 tsp thyme
1 tsp basil
1 tsp sage
1 Tbsp olive Oil
1 cup gratted cheese

MASHED POTATOES
3-4 russet potatoes
½ cup milk
¼ cup butter

In a large skillet brown the ground beef and ground lamb, add salt and pepper.
When cooked drain excess fat.
In a separate skillet, cook onions in olive oil and add thyme, basil, sage. Continue to cook until onions are soft and translucent. Add tomato paste to onions and spices, then add this mixture to the meat and combine throughly.
Mix Bisto Powder, beef base, and hot water together; add this and the Worcestershire to the skillet.
Bring mixture to a boil then reduce heat and simmer gently for approximately 45 mins.
Add diced carrots and peas, bring back to a boil, and simmer for 1 hour.

Mashed Potatoes

Peel and quarter potatoes. Boil potatoes thouroughly.
In large bowl mash potatoes while adding milk, butter, salt and pepper to taste.

Remove from heat and transfer to a large casserole dish or baking pan. Top with mashed potatoes, grated cheese, and breadcrumbs. Run under broiler to just barely brown the crust, and serve with mash potato and chedder cheese.

SHEPARDS PIE is "a traditional Irish dish that should be on every Irish restaurant menu. Most American-Irish restaurants have Americanized it by eliminating the lamb, but I believe it is a key ingredient that is a complete necessity in making a traditional 'Sheppard's' Pie. Using frozen peas and carrots makes sure your veggies don't get soggy during the simmering time."
— *Tommy, executive chef, Flanagan's*

BISTO POWDER is a gravy powder that browns, seasons and thickens to create a traditional style homemade gravy. It's a way to have a traditional gravy for your dishes without actually making it from scratch.

PARK CITY, UTAH

福

FLYING SUMO SUSHI & GRILL

OM

The Flying Sumo has been a Park City tradition now for 18 years, providing top-quality seafoods and sushi in an inviting and relaxed atmosphere, with unpretentious great service, and friendly chefs.

Patrons know that they always receive the freshest fish, quality ingredients, mixed with home cooking, at reasonable prices. The Flying Sumo is one of the most consistent and best restaurants in Park City.

It all started with the Happy Sumo restaurant about 20 years ago; one of the first sushi places in town, before any sort of sushi trend. After 8 years of operation two brothers bought Happy Sumo and changed the name to Flying Sumo, the restaurant was then purchased by a Korean couple 8 years after that. In 2011 the current owner, Emerson Oliveira of The Bridge Cafe, bought Flying Sumo. Emerson has retained all of the traditional, popular, and successful dishes, and every year is adding a few more rolls.

Start off with some fragrant miso soup and edamame, before ordering from the deep menu. In addition to traditional Nigiri, Uramaki, Hosomaki, and Sashimi rolls, specialty rolls are very popular. For example, the Tropic Thunder combines coconut shrimp, avocado and cucumber, rolled in soy paper. Or perhaps the Jessica Albacore will attract you with its tuna, cucumbers, radish sprouts, albacore, and garlic ginger. The whimsical names will make you smile, but you'll break into a broad grin when you taste them.

For the sushi-shy members of your group, there's the teriyaki bowl, curry, or chicken skewers (Yakitori), and a kid's menu for this family friendly, and fun, spot.

SUSHI CHEF ADAM BROWN

Chef Adam Brown grew up in Tucson, Arizona, and has been in restaurants since 1992.

With deep experience in fine dining and other culinary genres, he began preparing sushi in 2003.

Since then Chef Brown has refined his style, combining the traditional with the contemporary at Flying Sumo. He assures all patrons that the quality will be unexcelled, and that all dishes are prepared with meticulous care, on a personal level.

The Flying Sumo is energetic and lively, but not too loud; a great combination for a resort town, and locals, crowd.

Whether you're ordering the Chuck Norris roll or the more traditional Sashima, Brown promises that you will enjoy the experience, the food, and the restaurant. And he knows you'll be back again.

PG56 PG57 PG58

Tokyo Nachos

2 cups daikon radish, shredded into long strands
8 Tbsp finely chopped raw sushi-grade tuna
6 tsp finely sliced scallions
1 tsp sesame oil
2 Tbsp sriracha

2 tsp Japanese mayonnaise
  (such as Kewpie brand)
3-4 dashes Japanese 7-spice powder
  (togarashi)
vegetable oil for deep-frying

8 japanese wontons
8 thin slivers avocado
½ cup kaiware
4 tsp tobiko
ponzu sauce, for garnish

Place the radish strands in a bowl of ice water for 30 minutes, changing the water after 15 minutes.
Drain well and set aside.
Prepare a spicy tuna mixture by combining the tuna, 2 teaspoons of scallions, sesame oil, mayonnaise, sriracha and japanese 7-spice powder (togarashi) in a small bowl. Set aside in the refrigerator.
Heat the vegetable oil to 350 degrees in a deep-fryer and fry wonton wrapper for about 30 seconds, or until crunchy. Drain on a paper towel. Repeat with other wonton.
Assemble the "nachos" on a large platter, and position the radish strands as a nest on which the nachos will rest.

Spread the fried wonton on top of the radish strands in an even layer.
Top each wonton with 1 tablespoon of the spicy tuna mixture and a sliver of avocado.
Garnish each "nacho" with ½ teaspoon of tobiko and ½ teaspoon of the scallions. Finish with a drop of ponzu sauce at the center of each "nacho."

This top selling appetizer at Flying Sumo will have you craving for more. The representation of a Mexican nacho in a more upscale view with Japanese fresh tuna and a slice of avocado makes Tokyo Nachos a locals and visitor favorite appetizer.

TOBIKO, the Japanese word for the flying fish roe is most widely known for its use in creating certain types of sushi.
The eggs are small, ranging from 0.5 to 0.8 mm. For comparison, tobiko is larger than masago (capelin roe), but smaller than ikura (salmon roe). Natural tobiko has a red-orange color, a mild smoky or salty taste, and a crunchy texture.

Sometimes tobiko is colored to change its appearance, other natural ingredients are used to accomplish the change, such as squid ink to make it black, yuzu to make it pale orange (almost yellow), or even wasabi to make it green and spicy. Sometimes a serving of tobiko contains several pieces, each having a different color.

KAIWARE are sprouted daikon radish seeds. They have a powerful radish flavor with a real peppery finish. You can find them in Asian grocery stores. They are sold usually in little clumps with the roots attached.

PONZU SAUCE is a tart citrus based sauce used in Japanese cuisine.

Coconut Chicken Curry

3 chicken breasts, sliced into tenders
1 Tbsp butter or coconut oil
1 cup coconut cream (skim from the top of 1 refrigerated can (13.5oz) of coconut milk)
1 cup chicken broth or stock
2 cup diced carrots

1 cup chopped celery
2 tomatoes, diced
1½ Tbsp curry powder or garam masala
1 Tbsp fresh ginger, grated
½ Tbsp sugar
¼ cup cilantro, coarsely chopped

6 garlic cloves, minced
1 Tbsp soy sauce
1 Tbsp freshly squeezed lime juice
salt and pepper to taste

Sauté the chicken with butter, or coconut oil in a medium-sized saucepan.

When the outside of the chicken has all turned white, add in the coconut cream and the chicken broth and mix well.

Add in the carrots, celery, and tomatoes.

Add in the ginger and curry powder (or garam masala).

Cook on medium heat with the lid on for 15 minutes, stirring occasionally.

Add the minced garlic and cilantro, salt to taste, and finish with dash of sugar, soy and lime.

Cook for another 2 minutes and serve with rice.

The Coconut Chicken Curry at Flying Sumo is served with the right amount of heat, with a great combination of flavors. You'll think twice about just having sushi.

F-N Jam Roll

OM | **E**

2 shrimp
3 oz Hamachi (yellowtail)
1 cup flour
1 cup shaved coconut
sushi rice
Japanede rice vinegar

1 sheet soy paper
1 sheet nori (dried seaweed)
2 slices avocados
2 oz crab meat
3 shishitos peppers
1 jalapeno, diced

½ habanero, diced
1 oz cilantro, chopped
1 Tbsp fresh squeezed lime juice
2 oz May Ploy sweet chili sauce

Coconut Shrimp
Roll 2 fresh shrimp on a bed of flour then on a bed of shaved coconut.
Deep fry until golden brown. Let rest on a paper.

Roll
Use a rice cooker, if available, (high quality brand sushi rice), place cooked rice in a flat bowl and add Japanese rice vinegar, let it cool down. Boil and cook sushi rice as directed on package.
Steam or boil crab meat to cook thoroughly, approximately 5 minutes.

Jam Sauce:
In a bowl mix jalapeno, habanero, cilantro, lime juice and may ploy sweet chili sauce.
Let it rest in the refrigerator.

On a shushi mat lay down the soy paper.
Add a layer of sushi rice.
Lay down the nori on top of the rice, two coconut shrimp, three shishitos, hamachi (yellowtail), avocado, crab, roll, cut.
Add jam sauce, diced jalapeno and habanero (less haba) cilantro, lime juice and May Ploy sweet chili mix.
Sprinkle across top of roll

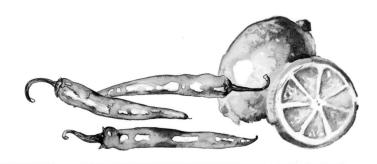

SHISHITO PEPPER *This Japanese pepper is finger-long, and slender. It turns red upon ripening but is usually harvested while green. While it's primarily a sweet, East Asian pepper, one of every 10 peppers is spicy.*

HAMACHI *as it is known in Japan is also known as the Japanese amberjack or yellowtail. Native to and mainly found in in the norethwest Pacific Ocean, from Japan to Hawaii.*

GATEWAY GRILLE

K

SEAN WHARTON

Just a 15 minute drive away from the buzzing clamor of Park City, drive over to the small-town American town of Kamas. It's a beautiful journey, but the Gateway Grill is the destination. The town is aptly named for the Gateway to the Uinta Mountains, and you'll need to stop for a hearty breakfast before you head up high, or for fine dining after the day is done. The outdoor patio is a cool and calming refuge after a long day.

American Airlines magazine described it: " We are talking four star phenomenal food at competitive prices in this tiny little town." Open all day for breakfast, lunch, and dinner, it's a combination of family restaurant and fine dining. Everyone will be able to find something to write home about, whether it's the eleven types of hamburgers, a rack of lamb, or butternut squash soup that is just too good. The menu ranges from steaks, to seafood, to pasta, to Mexican dishes.

You'll compete for space with local ranchers, fishermen, and visitors for comfort foods like chicken fried steak and mashed potatoes. Sports cars squeeze in between the big pickup trucks. Make your breakfast the biscuits and gravy, or the Grande burrito. If you can't get enough of the buttermilk syrup, they'll give you the recipe. Lunch ranges from smoked chicken wings, to a salmon sandwich, or fire roasted veggie panini.

Start your dinner with the artichoke bruschetta or calamari rings, then dine on the 14-ounce blackened rib eye steak, or the double cut pork chop, paired with a fine Argentinian Malbec. Or try a down home dish like shepherd's pie, or the grilled ribs. Follow that with a piece of raspberry white chocolate cheesecake, the cream brulee, or key lime pie to finish.

Gateway Grille does take reservations, so head towards this fine restaurant in this two-stoplight town. It's worth the journey.

Sean and Rebecca Wharton opened the Gateway Grill in 1997 in what was once a burger and shake shack, complete with a drive-in window.

Sean spent over a dozen years overseeing the world-famous Seafood Buffet at Deer Valley, before starting his own place. During the off season he would head to the New Jersey coast's restaurant 410 Bank Street to hone his skills, and brushed up on his techniques at the Culinary Institute of America in Hyde Park, New York.

As a caterer, Wharton has prepared meals for Presidents Clinton and Bush, as well as luminaries such as Richard Dreyfus, Stephen Spielberg, and Mitt Romney. Together Sean and Rebecca have created a dining refuge in Kamas, and they'll welcome you to the "other side" of Summit County with a fine meal.

PG64   PG65   PG66

Grilled Ahi Tuna Tower with Roasted Pepper Salad and Cucumber Wasabi Guacamole

6 tuna steaks
1 lrg red pepper, roasted, peeled and chopped
1 lrg yellow pepper, roasted, peeled and chopped
2 roma tomatoes, seeded and julienned
2 cremini mushrooms, sliced
¼ small red onion, julienned

2 Tbsp green onions, chopped
2 Tbsp basil, julienned
3 Tbsp extra virgin olive oil
3 Tbsp balsamic vinegar
1 tsp ground garlic
salt and pepper to taste

GUACAMOLE
2 lrg avocados, peeled
¼ bunch of cilantro, chopped
½ cup of cucumber peeled, diced, and seeded
2 Tbsp wasabi powder
3 Tbsp rice wine vinegar

Salad

In a mixing bowl, combine the red and yellow peppers, tomatoes, mushrooms, onions, and basil. In a small bowl add the olive oil, balsamic vinegar and garlic, mix well and add to the vegetable mix. Season to taste with salt and pepper. Let stand 30 minutes before serving for flavors to mix.

Guacamole

In a small mixing bowl, combine avocados, chopped cilantro, diced and seeded cucumber, wasabi powder and rice wine vinegar. Mash all ingredients together with a fork. Season to taste with salt and pepper.

Tuna

Cut fish into 3-4 oz medallions. Lightly season with your favorite spice oil. Grill to medium rare.

Assembly

On top of your favorite risotto place first layer of tuna, then place the a portion of the pepper salad on top of the tuna, repeat with another layer of tuna, then top with guacamole. Serve with your favorite risotto and vegetables.

Serves 6

Roasted Butternut Squash Soup with Pecan and Maple Cream

4 butternut squash, peeled and diced
1 small white onion, diced
2 garlic cloves
8 cups chicken stock
1 cup heavy cream
1 Tbsp salt
1 tsp cumin ground

MAPLE CREAM
½ cup sour cream
¼ cup pecans, toasted and chopped
2 Tbsp maple syrup

Preheat the oven to 375 degrees.
Lightly oil a large baking pan.
Peel and dice the butternut squash and white onion.
Season the squash, onions and garlic with salt and pepper.
Roast in oven for 1 hour or until lightly brown and soft to the touch.
Remove from oven, put the squash, onion, and garlic in a medium sauce pan and cover with chicken stock and heavy cream.
Bring to a light simmer, then puree until smooth.
Season to taste.

Maple Cream
Mix together the sour cream and maple syrup.
Toast and finely chop the pecans and add to sour cream and maple syrup mixture.
Mix and use to garnish soup before serving.

Key Lime Pie

K | D

1 10 inch graham cracker pie crust
1 14 oz can of sweetened condensed milk
2 limes, zest

3 egg yolks
½ cup fresh squeezed lime juice
16 oz cream cheese softened

Preheat oven to 350°.
In a medium mixing bowl, combine the milk, lime zest, fresh squeezed lime juice, the 3 egg yolks and cream cheese, mix on high until thick and smooth.

Pour into the pie crust and bake for 15-20 minutes.
Refrigerate for 2 hours before serving.
Top with whipped cream.

THE KEY LIME is an American dessert made from key limes rather than regular limes. Key limes which are more tart and aromatic than regular limes and the juice is pale yollow, not your usual green colored juice of limes, hence the yellow color of the pie filling. The dish is named after the small Key limes that are native throughout the Florida Keys.

The thickening agent in the pie is due to the reaction when mixing the condensed milk and the acidic lime juice which eliminates the need for baking to thicken and made it easy in early days to make the pie anywhere since there was no need to bake.
Today, key lime pies are cooked are usually baked for a short time because consuming raw eggs is considered dangerous. The baking also thickens the texture more than the reaction alone.

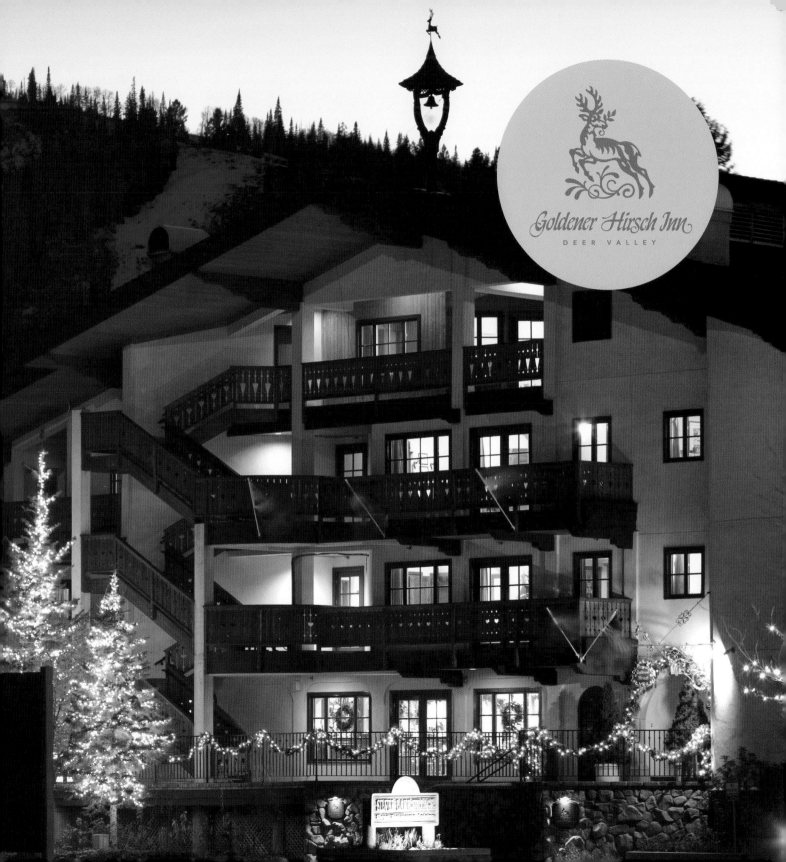

Goldener Hirsch Inn

DEER VALLEY

GOLDENER HIRSCH INN

SL

CHEF RYAN

The Goldener Hirsch Inn, though modeled after its 600 year old namesake in Salzburg, Austria, is unique to America and to Park City. It's a cozy refuge from bustling Deer Valley Resort at Silver Lake, with comfy rooms, great dining, and authentic European decor. It's the only family-owned hotel in Deer Valley. And, while it's not just a few steps to Beethoven's House, like its namesake, it is just a few steps away from some of the world's finest skiing. As for dining, it's a AAA-Four Diamond experience with award-winning menus and a superb wine cellar.

At the Goldener Hirsch, guests are treated like family and, in fact the, rooms have been decorated by owner Spence Eccles' family. Celebrating their 25th anniversary t his year, the hotel boasts one and two bedroom suites with feather beds, each opened with an antique, large brass key. There are private balconies, wood burning fireplaces, and large living areas, plus cookies and hot chocolate every afternoon. There's even a pull-rope bell on the front balcony to ring in special occasions.

According to Excecutive Chef Ryan Burnham, they have a lot of repeat business. "It's a great place for après ski in the winter, and a perfect place to get a proper meal." The service is perfect, the waiters attentive, but not overbearing. It's Austrian elegance at its finest and most luxurious.

The cuisine is contemporary European alpine, with an American spin, changed seasonally to reflect local ingredients. Start off with the fondue, porcini mushroom soup, or artichoke risotto, then on to an authentic Wiener schnitzel, gnocchi, or Niman Ranch lamb, all accompanied with unique sides such as blue corn grits, chimmichurri, or spaetzle. There's a lovely, south-facing private room perfect for celebrations, dinners, and events, or attend one of the wine or beer dinners. There's also a full service catering department, and of course room service if you're just too wiped out from a full day on the mountain. The attention to detail is a nice surprise, with hand painted walls, alpenhorns, and hand-carved chairs. It's a mix of European elegance with a homey feel. No wonder that in 2013 it was voted as the United States' Best Ski Boutique Hotel.

This will be Executive Chef Ryan Burnham's fourth winter at the Goldener Hirsch. He came to Park City via Alta, Utah, Washington DC, San Francisco, and Florida. "I've had the opportunity to reopen a few very nice hotel restaurants," he says, "including the Clift Hotel in San Francisco, and the Fontainebleau in Florida."

What's he like best about his work? "I love the contact I have with everyone, from the farmers to the cooks to the owners to the guests, "he says. "It's the closest thing to team sports for an adult." He has a great gift for unique combinations and fresh variations, something he might pass along to his 2-year-old daughter, Tevie, some day.

He's always learning and trying new techniques which he shares with his guests. "We cook with the season too, "he says, of sourcing ingredients from nearby farms when possible. "We cook with a lot of flavor. But not with a lot of butter. We keep your health in mind." His stellar beef, pork chops, and fish entrees, fine breads and pastries, unique soups, and signature fondue will satisfy even the most discriminating pallet, and the hungriest skier.

PG72   PG73   PG74

Goldener Hirsch Cheese Fondue

1 cup dry white wine	1oz Kirsch	SLURRY
2 cloves garlic, minced	small pinch nutmeg	corn starch
3 oz Appenzeller cheese, grated	salt & pepper to taste	water
2 oz Emmentaller cheese, grated	2 Granny Smith apples, sliced or cubed	
2 oz Vacherin cheese, grated	½ broccoli	
1 oz cave aged Gruyere cheese, grated	baguette, or bread of choice, cubed	

In a fondue pot, warm the white wine with the garlic over medium heat.

While this is heating make your slurry. Mix together equal parts water and cornstarch, blend well and set aside.

To the fondue pot, slowly add the cheeses, Kirsch and salt and pepper.

Increase the heat to melt the cheese.

Finally, add the slurry slowly (an ounce at a time) until you have stabilized the mixture to the desired consistency, so it does not separate.

Serve the fondue with crusty bread, broccoli and Granny Smith apples. Or dip lemony potatoes, sliced bratwurst or even schnitzel when those are on hand.

Serves 2-4 people.

FONDUE is an Italian, Swiss and French dish of melted cheese in a communal pot over a candle or spirit lamp. Bread and other items are dipped into the cheese using a long-stemmed fork. Chefs at the Goldener Hirsch start grating cheese well before the ski season to meet the demand. They will go through over 500 pounds of cheese over the Christmas holiday.

KIRSCH is a clear, colorless fruit brandy. It is traditionally made by double distilling morello cherries, a dark-colored sour cherry that produces a less sweet brandy. Today, it is also made from other kinds of cherries. Kirsch is made from the whole cherry, including the pits which is what gives kirsch a bitter-almond taste.

Niman Ranch 'Tomahawk' Pork Chop

PORK BRINE
1 pork chop, per person
½ cup salt
1 cup pure maple syrup
2 garlic cloves, crushed
1 inch knob of ginger
2 Tbsp chopped rosemary
2 Tbsp chopped thyme
½ tsp allspice

ARUGULA PISTOU
1 cup blanched arugula
4 Tbsp lemon juice
⅓ cup toasted almonds
1/3 cup parmesan cheese
4 garlic cloves
1 cup extra virgin olive oil
salt & pepper to taste

GARDEN SUCCOTASH
1 cup corn, removed from cob
¼ cup fresh peas
¼ cup heirloom tomatoes, diced
¼ cup roasted peppers, diced
2 Tbsp lemon juice
2 Tbsp extra virgin olive oil

BLUE CORN GRITS
4 cups blue grits
1 gallon stock, chicken or vegetable
1 quart heavy cream
3 cups cheddar cheese
½ cup butter
salt & pepper to taste

SHERRY VINEGAR JUS
4 lbs pork butt, fat trimmed,
  cut into large chunks
1 large onion, chopped
1 large carrot, chopped

1 large celery stalk, chopped
1 head garlic, cut in half
1 Tbsp coriander seeds
1 Tbsp fennel seeds
½ bunch fresh sage
1 cup quality sherry vinegar
1 gallon veal stock

SWISS CHARD
2 bunches swiss chard
1 gallon water
3 T butter
Salt & Pepper

Pork
In a saucepan, combine 5 cups of water, salt and maple syrup. Simmer to dissolve salt and syrup. Pull off the heat and add garlic, ginger, rosemary, thyme and allspice. Allow mixture to cool to room temperature. Place pork chops in brine for at least 4 hours, no longer than 12 hours.

Arugula Pistou
Combine blanched arugula, lemon juice, toasted almonds, parmesan cheese, garlic cloves, and extra virgin olive oil in a blender, then strain through a fine mesh sieve. Add salt & pepper to taste.

Garden Succotash
Combine corn kernnels, fresh peas, heirloom tomatoes, diced roasted peppers, lemon juice, and virgin olive oil; let set overnight.

Blue Corn Grits
Soak grits in enough water to cover for 2 hours, skimming any bits that float to the top. In a large stock pot, bring the stock and cream to a simmer. Add grits and cook over medium heat stirring every few minutes, making sure the grits don't burn on the bottom. Cook until grits are tender, about 1 hour. Finish with the cheese, butter, salt and pepper.

Swiss Chard
Remove the stalks, and chop the leaves. In boiling water add a generous pinch of salt and submerge the leaves for 1 minute. Meanwhile, warm the butter in a saute pan. Add the wilted chard to the warmed butter, and season with salt and pepper.

Sherry Vinegar Jus
Season pork and roast in oven on high heat until brown and just cooked. In a heavy bottomed sauce pot, sweat the onion, carrot, celery, garlic, coriander seeds, fennel seeds and fresh sage until soft. Add the sherry vinegar and reduce by half. Add the veal stock and roasted pork, simmer until the liquid is reduced by half. Season the liquid with salt and pepper and strain.

Grill the pork chops. Top with the arugula pistou, serve with succotash, grits and Swiss chard, with sherry vinegar jus on the side.

Goldener Hirsch Apple Strudel

STRUDEL DOUGH
3 eggs
2oz canola oil
2 cups water
4½ cups flour
3 tsp salt

STRUDEL FILLING
10 lbs IQF (pre-sliced) granny smith apples
2 lbs brown sugar
4 each cinnamon sticks
2 cups apple cider
1½ Tbsp vanilla extract
1 lemon, zested
½ cup golden raisins
1 cup dried cranberries

CIDER CARAMEL
1 gallon apple cider
4 cinnamon sticks
6 cloves
1 Tbsp butter
½ cup brown sugar

Strudel Dough

In a large mixer, whisk together eggs, oil and water. Add flour and salt.

With the paddle attachment, mix on low until a dough forms. On medium speed, mix until the dough wraps itself completely around the paddle, about 8 to 10 minutes.

On a generously oiled sheet tray, spread the dough into a square shape, taking care not to tear it. Lightly coat the dough in oil, and wrap with plastic wrap.

Refrigerate for at least 4 hours, or overnight preferably.

Strudel Filling

In a large sauce pan or stock pot, reduce the apple cider by half.

Add the sugar, vanilla, raisins, cranberries and lemon zest. Simmer until the fruit bursts. Add the apples and cook until semi soft.

Strain the mixture, reserving the liquid. Reduce the liquid by half, thicken with a slurry (cornstarch + water). Chill the fruit mixture and liquid separately overnight. Mix the following day.

Cider Caramel

In a heavy bottomed sauce pot, reduce the cider with the cinnamon sticks, and cloves by half and strain. In a separate saucepan, caramelize the sugar with the butter. Add the reduced cider, simmer and strain.

To assemble the strudel, portion the dough into 4 portions. Over a floured work surface, hand stretch the dough until it is a translucent rectangle, taking care not to tear it. Brush the dough with melted butter.

On the bottom 3 inches of dough, spread toasted breadcrumbs along the length of the dough. Add the filling on top of the toasted breadcrumbs, and roll forward.

Brush the top of the dough with more melted butter, then roll again. Brush the top of the dough with butter again then fold again. The last fold does not require the butter.

Bake in a pre-heated 375 degree oven for 10 minute, rotate the strudel, cook for 10 more minutes. Cut into large pieces, then dust with powdered sugar. Serve with the cider caramel sauce and ice cream.

Makes 2 logs, each serves 4-6 people

good karma

INDO-PERSIAN CUISINE WITH
PASSION AND INTEGRITY

GOOD KARMA

P

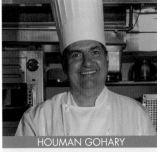

HOUMAN GOHARY

Good Karma Restaurant has proudly been serving Indian-Persian-influenced cuisine since 2006. Good Karma restaurant is known best for the signature Morgan Valley Lamb curry, free-range chicken kebabs, and vegan and gluten-free entrees. Chef-Owner Houman Gohary (featured on the *Today Show* with Katie Couric during the 2002 Olympics, and in 2015 on Beat Bobby Flay show on *Food Network channel*) brings his 35 years of culinary experience to create unique farm-to-fork and flavorful dishes. Chef Gohary believes that taste is the sauce of joy and love and that it is an instrument to good health and happiness.

Good Karma's sister company, Instant Karma, founded by Blanca Gohary, makes and distributes all-natural, ready-to-eat, whole, flavorful food items that are vegan and gluten-free. Good Karma Restaurant and Instant Karma use the freshest ingredients and strive to buy local whenever possible to bring you "Indo-Persian cuisine with passion and integrity."

Chef Gohary came to Park City as part of the opening food and beverage team for Vail Resorts at Canyons. At Grand Summit lodge, he helped host the 2002 Winter Olympics as a Host Chef on NBC's *Today Show* with Katie Couric and Matt Lauer. Chef Gohary has also appeared on the Discovery Channel, PBS, and *The Food Network Channel* with Rachael Ray, and Food Fighters.

Gohary says, "My inspiration of cooking started at age of 7 when I used to go shopping with my grandmother 'Nushi' at the daily farmers' market. Supermarkets were non existent 45 years ago in my home town of Teheran. Processed chicken? Are you kidding me! I used to chase chicken feathers in our yard when the wind blew! I learned so much during that summer with my grandmother at age 7; more than 5 years of professional cooking school in Europe, 3 years in ACF and 2 years at The Culinary Institute of America in Hyde Park New York. Spend more time in selection than cooking, she used to always say. Selection, Selection, Selection."

Chef Houman Gohary's culinary training is in classical French and Austrian pastries. After perfecting and blending fusion dishes for years, Chef Gohary returned to his Persian roots of purity and simplicity. His mission is to supply bold flavors, small bites that are healthy, and farm to table cuisine for the discriminating global traveler, athletic individual and health-minded lifestyle of our local community.

Chef Gohary's signature dishes are pure and exotic. He utilizes organic, local and seasonal products whenever possible. He looks forward to sharing his talent and knowledge of unique vegan and gluten free recipes with Park City locals, visitors and other local chefs. Houman volunteers his time and the restaurant's capacity for local community events, fund raising activities, cooking class, as well as private functions for higher education.

PG80 PG81 PG82 PG83

Shrimp Vindaloo Salad

1 lb 16/20 count/lb shrimp,
  peel and deveined
1 lb assorted baby vegetables, thinly sliced

VINDALOO SAUCE
1½ cups onion, chopped
4 tsp fresh ginger, minced
3 cloves garlic, minced
¼ cup jalapeño peppers, chopped
4 cups tomatoes, peeled, seeded and chopped
½ cup tomato paste
½ tsp paprika
½ tsp coriander, ground
½ tsp cumin, ground

½ tsp turmeric, ground
½ tsp cayenne pepper, ground
½ tsp cinnamon, ground
⅛ tsp cloves, ground
⅛ tsp cardamom, ground
1 Tbsp red wine vinegar
1 Tbsp olive oil
1 cup coconut milk
salt and pepper to taste

Vindaloo Sauce

In a small bowl combine the paprika, coriander, cumin, turmeric, ground cayenne pepper, cinnamon, cardamom, and cloves.
Add the red wine vinegar and stir to form a paste. Set aside.
Heat the oil in a nonstick skillet over medium-high heat.
Add the chopped onions and cook for 2 minutes or until they are soft and translucent.
Add jalapeno, minced ginger and garlic to the onions and cook for 1 minute.
Add tomatoes and tomato paste and simmer for 5 minutes.
Add spice paste and cook gently 10 minutes, stirring constantly.
Stir in coconut milk and ground cardamom.
Peel and devein the shrimp and add to the sauce and cook for 5 minutes or until shrimp are done and turn bright orange, stirring occasionally.

Taste and adjust the seasoning with salt and pepper.
Place the sauce on the bottom of the plate or platter, arrange the shrimp on the top and garnish with thinly sliced baby vegetables around the shrimp.

Serves 6 to 8

VINDALOO is a fiery spice blended from coriander, garlic, cumin, ginger, cinnamon, crushed brown mustard, cayenne, jalapeno pepper, cardamom, turmeric, black pepper and cloves.

Chef Gohary philosophy is never compromise quality and taste. Chef Gohary believes that taste is the sauce of joy and love and it is an instrument to happiness and good health.

Persian Chicken Kebab with Saffron Rice and Raita

2 lbs skinless, boneless organic chicken breast,
  trimmed cut into 1" cubes
½ cup olive oil
1 large yellow onion, sliced
¼ cup garlic, sliced
1 tsp saffron, ground with sugar
1 tsp sumac
  (Persian spice from dried berries)
1 tsp turmeric
1 lime, juiced

1 lemon, juiced
¼ cup flat parsley, chopped
¼ cup mint, chopped
1 tsp salt
1 tsp freshly cracked pepper
1 red onion
1 green bell pepper
1 yellow bell pepper
8 wooden skewers soaked in cold water
  (or metal skewers)

PERSIAN SAFFRON RICE
2 cups water
3 cups basmati rice
¼ cup plus 2 tsp clarified butter
1 Tbsp salt
2 tsp whole milk yogurt
¼ Tbsp turmeric
¼ Tbsp saffron
1 tsp sugar
¼ cup hot water

Place a grill plate on the burner over medium heat.

In a large bowl mix together the olive oil, sliced onion, garlic, mint, parsley, lime, lemon juice, turmeric and ground saffron. Season the cubed chicken with salt and pepper then thoroughly coat with the herb and onion mixture.

Cut the peppers and red onion into 2 inch squares and set aside.

Remove the skewers from the water. Gently alternate the peppers, onions and six pieces of chicken onto each skewer. Grill over medium heat turning often until brown, about 5 minutes on each side. Sprinkle the kebabs with sumac. Serve over Persian saffron rice or pita bread.

Persian Saffron Rice

Rinse rice in cold water until water is clear.

Parboil the rice in salted water for 5 minutes until the outer layer of the rice is soft but the center is firm.

Drain the rice with a fine-mesh sieve and let it air dry for few minutes.

In a mixing bowl, grind the saffron, sugar and turmeric together in a mortar and mix with the hot water to extract the color and flavor.

Add the saffron mixture to the rice and mix gently until the color is light orange.

For the rice crust (Tadigh), combine one cup of the parboiled saffron rice with the yogurt and set aside.

Heat a heavy bottom pan or muffin tin (for individual portions).

Add the clarified butter to the pan and cover just the bottom of the pan with the rice-yogurt mixture.

Gently layer the rest of the rice to the pan little at the time along with the salt and 2 teaspoons of the butter. Cook the rice on medium heat for 5 minutes to form the rice crust (Tadigh) then turn down to low heat.

Cover the lid of the pan with a towel and cover the pan to hold the moisture. Continue cooking at low heat about 30 minutes or until the rice is tender.

After the rice is cooked, invert the rice in a round platter. The rice should come out like a round cake with a golden crust on the top.

For individual rice in muffin tins, make sure the rice is not sticking by gently remove the rice by running your knife or spatula along the side of the muffin tins Remove from the pan and serve hot with yogurt or Shish Kebab.

Serves 6 to 8
Raita recipe on page 82

Tandoori Lamb Shish Kebab
with Saffron Rice and Raita

2 lbs boneless local leg of lamb (not frozen),
   trimmed, cut into 1" cubes
½ cup olive oil
1 large yellow onion, grated
¼ cup garlic, minced
1 Tbsp tomato paste
1 Tbsp garam masala seasoning
1 Tbsp sumac (Persian spice from dried berries)
1 tsp turmeric
1 lime, juiced

¼ cup house-made yogurt
   (or whole milk yogurt)
¼ cup chopped flat parsley
1 tsp salt
1 tsp freshly cracked pepper
1 red onion
1 green bell pepper
1 yellow bell pepper
8 wooden skewers soak in
   cold water (or metal skewer)

RAITA
2 cups plain yogurt
1 large english cucumber
¼ cup red onion (diced)
1 tsp ground cumin
¼ cup mint leaves (chopped)
salt and pepper to taste

Place a grill plate on the burner over medium heat.

In a large bowl, mix together oil, tomato paste, yogurt, grated onion, garlic, chopped parsley, lime juice, garam masala and turmeric. Season the cubed lamb with salt and pepper. Add the seasoned lamb to the tomato paste mixture and combine well, making sure the lamb is coated with the mixture thoroughly.

Cut the peppers and red onion into 2 inch squares and set aside. Remove the skewers from the water and gently skewer the peppers, onions and six pieces of lamb onto each skewer. Make sure you alternate the vegetables and meat for color and texture.

Grill the kebabs on medium heat, turning them often until brown about 5 minutes on each side.

Sprinkle the kebabs with sumac after they are cooked to desired temperature.

Serve over saffron basmati rice or pita bread.

Raita (cucumber and yogurt sauce)

Season yogurt with the salt and cumin.
Cut the cucumber in half, remove the seeds.
Grate the cucumber and red onion together with a grater then add to yogurt mixture. Mix well.
Sprinkle the mint on the top and serve.

Serves 6 to 8

Saffron rice recipe on page 81

SUMAC *a Persian spice from the dried berries of the sumac bush. Native to the Middle East, the sumac bush produces deep red berries. For the the sumac spice the berries are dried and ground into coarse powder. Ground sumac has a tangy lemony flavor but less tart than a real lemon.*

Saffron Rice Pudding

½ cup basmati rice
½ cup water
2 cups milk
2 cups coconut milk
1 cup sugar

¼ cup green raisins
1 tsp cardamom seeds
½ cup toasted almonds
6-8 drops rose water
¼ cup toasted pistachios or toasted almonds for garnish

Wash, rinse and drain the basmati rice with cold water until the water runs clear.

Soak in ½ cup water for ½ hour.

Combine the rice and 4 cups of water in a heavy bottomed skillet. Gently simmer until the water evaporates and the rice is creamy.

Add the milk and continue to simmer on low heat until the rice becomes the consistency of porridge.

Stir occasionally at first and then constantly when the milk begins to thicken to keep from sticking to bottom of pot.

Add sugar, raisins, cardamom, rose water and almonds and continue to cook for additional 5 minutes.

Make sure to stir continuously to prevent the ingredients from sticking to the bottom of the pan.

After 5 minutes, remove from the heat and set aside to cool.

Taste and adjust the sweetness of the rice pudding to your personal taste.

Sprinkle with pistachios or almonds, serve chilled or warm in dessert bowls.

Serves 6

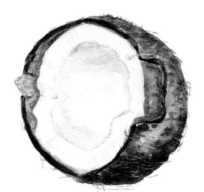

SAFFRON is harvested from the flower of the saffrom crocus, and is one of the most expensive spices in the world.

CHEF GOHARY says, "Most of these recipes reminds me of my roots and childhood in Teheran where I used to shop with my grandmother from farmers markets and eat street food from local vendors."

NO NAME SALOON AND GRILL

MS

This bar's motto is, "Helping people forget their names since 1903!" They're not kidding, 'cuz this is a bustling, loud meeting place for locals and tourists alike in the heart of Historic Main Street. Outside it's an ornate brick "Alamo" style building, inside it's old and rustic, where flowers grow out of old commodes, the ceiling looks like a yard sale and there are hanging collectibles throughout the entire place. The heated rooftop deck has a million-dollar view up and down Main Street, plus there are plenty of flat screens for all the games.

Not just a PBR and shot joint, although they sell a lot of both while patrons kick back and eat the Housemade Chips served with No Name Saloon Salsa. The No Name makes the best Buffalo Burgers this side of the Mississippi. The Saloon Burger is a "Burgerlicious nine napkin half pound monster," served with grilled onions, cheese, tomatoes, shredded lettuce and mayo. As the "Home of the Buffalo Burger", the No Name Saloon is the #1 purchaser of Buffalo meat in Utah. You don't want to miss these burgers.

You can also enjoy the Buffalo Nachos, with corn tortilla chips smothered in black beans, two types of cheese, pico de gallo, sour cream, guacamole, and of course ground buffalo meat. It's a real meal. Or try a basket of killer fish tacos while you listen to classic rock or watch your favorite sports.

"This bar's an oasis of leisure," said one visitor. It's the place where everyone unwinds and refuels. At the No Name, if you don't know everyone already, you soon will. It's that kind of place, and it's how the locals roll. You'll be back again and again.

Jose Cuellar's eyes sparkle as he talks of what he likes to cook. "I really like the winter mushroom buffalo, with huckleberry glaze," he says, "and, really, all of the wild game. I like to experiment."

After working with a variety of "schooled chefs", the realization of Jose's "real world" experiences put him into his executive role. His passion and attention to detail are demonstrated by the superb quality of his cuisine.

Chef Cuellar has been the head chef at Butcher's Chop House and Bar as well as at No Name Saloon and Grill for the past 6 years, but has been working at Butcher's since they opened 12 years ago. Butcher's is a big-city chop house, situated nicely in the middle of Park City's famous mountains. As a local son, Jose is doing exactly what he wants to do, where he wants to do it.

Buffalo Nachos

1 lb corn tortilla chips
1 lb ground buffalo meat
3 oz cooked black beans
2 oz pickled jalapeno slices
½ cup shredded monterey jack cheese
1 cup shredded yellow cheddar cheese
2 Tbsp sour cream
2 Tbsp guacamole
GUACAMOLE
6 avocados
1 bunch cilantro
½ red onion, diced

1 tomato
3 whole limes
salt and pepper to taste

PICO DE GALLO
4 tomato, diced
½ red onion, diced
½ bunch cilantro, chopped
1 jalapeno, dices
2 tsp lime juice
salt and pepper to taste

In a large skillet, brown buffalo meat and spoon over plated tortilla chips. Top with the black beans, then the sliced jalapenos and monterey jack and cheddar cheeses. Place in oven or broiler for 6-8 minutes or until cheese has melted. Remove from oven, top with sour cream, guacamole, and pico de gallo and serve.

Buffalo is our preference but you can substitute beef if you would like but we would rather you took some time to hunt the buffalo.

Guacamole
Cut avocados in half and take out seed. Place avocado in a medium bowl and mash gently for 3 minutes.
Add diced red onion, diced tomato, and chopped cilantro.
Add lime juice salt and pepper to taste.

Pico de Gallo
In a medium bowl, place diced tomato, diced red onion, chopped cilantro, and diced jalapenos. Mix well and add lime juice and salt, pepper to taste.

Turkey Burger

MS | **E**

1 lb ground turkey
½ tsp salt
½ tsp pepper

1 bunch cilantro chopped
2 slices cheddar or cheese of your choice
2 large lettuce leaves

1 ripe tomato, sliced
chips
2 floured burger buns

In a large bowl, hand mix ground turkey with salt, pepper and chopped cilantro. Hand form making two 8 oz patties.

On a flat grill or skillet, using a temp probe, cook patties through until internal temperature reaches 165 degrees top with cheddare cheese slice.

On burger buns of choice, place turkey patties and cheese along with lettuce and tomato, serve with chips or salad.

Here at the saloon, we use a lightly floured bun,
but feel free to use whatever bun you and your buddies prefer.

Serves 2

Fish Tacos

MS | **E**

2 - 3oz cod or halibut filets
   or choice of any white fish
2 oz shredded lettuce
2 6 inch Flour tortillas
½ cup canola oil

BEER BATTER
2 cans beer (we like PBR)
2 cups of flour

½ tsp chili powder
pinch garlic powder
salt and pepper to taste

CILANTRO CREAM SAUCE
1 cup Sour cream
2 oz fresh lime juice
1 bunch Cilantro
Salt & pepper to taste

PICO DE GALLO
4 tomatoes, diced
½ red onion, diced
½ bunch cilantro, chopped
1 jalapeno, diced
2 tsp lime juice
salt and pepper to taste

Beer Batter
Open both cans of beer, one for you and one for the fish. Wisk the flour, chili powder, garlic powder and salt and pepper with the 1 can of beer.
Rinse the fish and pat dry. Dip in batter to coat thoroughly. Heat the oil in a skilletl and pan fry the battered cod filets. Cut filets in half and place in tortillas. Top with shredded lettuce, pico de gallo and cilantro cream sauce.

Cilantro Cream Sauce
In a food processor add sour cream, lime juice, cilantro and salt & pepper. Blend for 3 minutes.

Pico de Gallo
In a medium bowl, place diced tomato, diced red onion, chopped cilantro, and diced jalapenos. Mix well and add lime juice and salt, pepper to taste.

park city
culinary institute
and event center

park city culinary institute
and event center

LAURIE MOLDAWER

PARK CITY CULINARY INSTITUTE
DV

This is where the most innovative and creative minds meet to share ideas, engage, inspire and entertain. Park City Culinary Institute collaborates with the region's top chefs to offer a distinctive culinary program that rivals some of the best culinary schools in the country. Small classes offer intimate exposure with notable, and often celebrity, chefs. Are you ready to impress your friends and family with your culinary skills? Learn knife skills that will rival your neighbors, and learn how to entice amazing flavors to work magic with your food. Park City Culinary Institute offers a unique opportunity to get hands-on experience in a real commercial kitchen in Deer Valley. People with all levels of experience are welcome and have attended our program, from beginners to professionals looking to advance their careers. Graduates range in age from 18 to over 60. The certificate program lasts just two months, and includes all of the fundamental techniques to cook like a pro.

The Park City Culinary Institute Event Center hosts teambuilding events, cooking demonstrations, and competitions for private and corporate groups. Our private dining facility hosts weddings, Bar Mitzvahs, executive retreats, and Sundance events. The Culinary Institute also offers distinctive off-site catering. Culinary Director Houman Gohary has appeared on the Food Network, NBC's Today Show and the Discovery Channel. An instructor at two prestigious culinary schools before joining Park City Culinary Institute, Houman was tapped by The Ritz Carlton resort group to train its food and beverage teams at international properties including, Shanghai, Barcelona, Dubai and Osaka. Other notable instructors on our faculty include Adam Kreisel, who has served as Executive Chef of The Tree Room at Sundance Resort, and the acclaimed Globe Café/by Moonlight; Greg Neville, the celebrated Executive Chef of Lugano Restaurant, recognized by Zagat's as one of America's Best Italian and awarded the Mobile Five Diamond Award, both Greg and Adam have cooked for the James Beard Foundation; and Chef Rebecca Millican, the Executive Pastry Chef at la Caille.

Park City Culinary Institute has been featured on Fox, ABC, and CBS (KUTV) for its innovative approach to culinary education. It opened a second campus in Salt Lake City in 2015.

Laurie started Park City Culinary Institute after attending culinary school in Paris, at le Cordon Bleu. She wanted to bring the European experience of culinary school to Park City, a town that has more chefs per capita than Paris! The school partners with experienced Executive Chefs, with an average of 20 years' experience to teach its programs.

A group of local farmers, cheese makers, bakers and chefs are turning the region into one of the hottest new culinary scenes. Field trips with Park City Culinary Institute include visits with Copper Moose Farm in Park City, Frog Bench Farms in Salt Lake City, and Zoe's Garden in Layton, Utah. Here in Park City, chefs not only work with farmers, but influence what farmers grow. The students also take field trips to learn how cheese is made, and how to make charcuterie.

PG96   PG97   PG98   PG99   PG100

park city culinary institute
— *and event center* —

Lobster Carpaccio

1½-2 Lb Maine lobsters, serves 2

LOBSTER TAPENADE
2 oz cooked lobster knuckle meat and
    tail trimmings
1 carrot stick, finely chopped
2 radishes, rinsed, trimmed and finely chopped
½ Tbsp green onions, chopped
½ Tbsp Italian parsley, finely chopped
¼ tsp fresh ginger, peeled and
    finely grated (microplane)
salt and pepper to taste
½ tsp fresh thyme
½ tsp capers, chopped
squeeze of lemon or orange
squeeze of vanilla bean olive oil

CARROT, RADISH AND GINGER PUREE
1 large carrot, peeled and chopped
4 radishes, rinsed, trimmed and chopped
2 garlic clove, chopped
1 Tbsp green onions, chopped (use the white
    part, save the green section for tapenade)
1 Tbsp fresh ginger, peeled and chopped
pinch of nutmeg
salt and pepper to taste
1 Tbsp butter
1 tsp fresh thyme
2 oz dry white wine
8 oz vegetable broth

**VANILLA BEAN EXTRA
VIRGIN OLIVE OIL**
1 vanilla bean, split and seeds
    scraped, reserve pod and seeds
¼ tsp orange zest
¼ tsp grated ginger
4 oz extra virgin olive oil
pinch of salt

GARNISH
orange & grapefruit sections,
    edible flowers, fresh thyme leaves,
    scallions, chives, lobster shell

Place live lobster in pot of boiling salted water. Cook lobster for exactly 6 minutes. Remove tail from head section and place in ice water bath. Place head and claw section back in boiling water for an additional 4 minutes. Remove from pot and add to ice water bath.

Place chilled lobster tail on cutting board upside down. Straighten tail and use scissors to cut the full length of the softer tail section shell. Try not to cut into meat. Spread shell and pull out entire lobster tail. Rinse under cold water to clean, pat dry. Reserve any trimmings for the tapenade. Reserve cov-

ered in refrigerator until ready to assemble. Remember, all of the lobster shells can be used to make a stock for other dishes. Pull the lobster claws off the head section. Place on cutting board. Cover claws with kitchen towel. Using a mallet, gently hit the lobster claws to crack the shell. Pull the claw meat from the shell carefully keeping the claw meat intact.

Check for cartilage in claw meat and remove. Use the same technique for the knuckles. Reserve extra knuckle and claw meat for the tapenade.

Continues on page 101

CHEF GREGORY NEVILLE *has won numerous accolades, including Best Chefs America, Best of State, Wine Spectator's Award of Excellence, and the Mobil Five Diamond Award. He was the Chef Owner of the acclaimed Lugano Restaurant in Salt Lake City, hailed in the Top 20 Restaurants of Utah* *by Zagat's, which also listed it as one of America's Best Italian Restaurants. Greg is a Certified Sommelier, and has cooked several times for the James Beard Foundation. Greg Neville joined the faculty of Park City Culinary Institute in 2015.*

park city culinary institute
— and event center —

Chawanmushi

(DV) (E)

1 organic chicken breast, cooked and chopped into small pieces
3 to 4 eggs (the ratio of eggs to dashi should be 1:3 by volume)
2 cups warm water
2 tsp dashi powder*
1 Tbsp mirin*

*If you can't find dashi powder or mirin, you can
use 2 cups of good chicken or mushroom broth*

1 dash sake
1 tsp soy sauce
2 shiitake mushrooms
umeboshi pickled plums, minced,
   or umeboshi plum paste
microgreens or green onions

In a small bowl, combine the water, dashi powder and mirin. Stir until dissolved.

In a medium bowl, gently whisk eggs with chopsticks while pouring in the dashi liquid and soy sauce, until completely blended.

Remove the pit and mince one umeboshi for each ramekin, a small amount of umeboshi paste will work as well. Sprinkle with microgreens, and add a few pieces of chicken and/or shiitake to each dish.

Pour the egg mixture into each bowl until nearly full. Use a strainer for the smoothest consistency.

In a large steamer or sauce pan, bring 1 inch of water to a boil. Reduce heat to a simmer and place ramekins, covered with aluminum foil, into the water. Steam on low heat for 12-15 minutes, or until the custard is firm but still somewhat soft and smooth.

The texture should be silky, and melt in your mouth. Garnish with shiitake mushrooms, stems removed, and sliced into strips. Serve warm.

Chawanushi

Chawanushi, translated means steamed tea cup, is a savory Japanese appetizer, similar to an egg flan. The flavors for this dish come from Dashi, Mirin and Soy. This is a lovely and relatively simple dish to make at home and can be made with chicken or shrimp, or a combination of both. Umeboshi pickled plums from an Asian market, and microgreens, are placed in the bottom of the ramekin to create a surprise flavor and texture with the first spoonful. If you can't find microgreens, green onions (scallions) will do the trick.

HOUMAN GOHARY Award-winning, innovative Chef Houman Gohary serves as the Culinary Director of Park City Culinary Institute. A key force in both the Southwestern and Spa Cuisine movements, Chef Gohary came to Utah to launch the food and beverage operations of the Canyons Resort when it first opened in 1999. Trained in Austria, and based in San Francisco for many years, Houman was appointed by the Ritz-Carlton to train the opening food and beverage teams at international properties. Two of those restaurants – the Ritz Carltons in Dubai and Osaka – were awarded the highly coveted three Michelin Stars.
You can regularly see Chef Gohary on The Food Network as both a

participant and judge. Houman has also been featured on NBC's Today Show and The Discovery Channel.

PROFESSIONAL TIP To bring out more flavor, toss the shiitake caps in a bit of grapeseed or pure olive oil, season them with salt and pepper, and roast them whole on a parchment-lined sheet pan in a 350 degree oven. When starting to caramelize and soften, remove them from the oven and let cool completely. Thinly slice the caps before adding to the ramekins.

park city culinary institute
— and event center —

Beet Gnocchi with Lemon Chèvre Cream

DV | E

BEET & RICOTTA GNOCCHI	1 Tbsp basil, finely chopped	10-12 pieces fennel, thin shaved	¼ cup shallots, finely minced
3-4 medium red beets	1 Tbsp parsley, finely chopped	4 oz candied walnuts	¼ cup sherry
1 small red beet	1 tsp kosher salt		½ cup vegetable stock
1 small yellow beet	¼ tsp white pepper	LEMON CHÈVRE CREAM	fresh lemon juice to taste
1 cup whole milk ricotta cheese	¾-1 cup all purpose flour	2 oz butter	4-6 oz chèvre (goat cheese)
1 large egg	½ cup grated parmesan cheese	1 Tbsp grapeseed oil	salt and white pepper to taste

Gnocchi

Roast medium red beets until tender, cool and put through a food processor. Roast the small red and yellow beets until tender, peel and set aside to garnish the sauce.

In a large bowl, combine the processed beets, ricotta and parmesan cheeses, egg, herbs, salt and pepper. Do not over mix. Slowly incorporate the flour, adding small amounts at a time until the mixture forms into a dough and is no longer wet. Add flour as needed to get to that stage. When you touch it, your finger should stay dry.

Add flour to your work surface to roll dough. Divide the dough into 4 equal pieces and roll them into long ropes – about 1 inch in diameter. Using a knife or bench scraper, cut the ropes into small, even pieces – about ½ inch thick. Place them onto a sheet pan lined with parchment paper dusted with flour.

At this point, you can flash freeze them to use later, or cook them immediately. To flash freeze, place inside a freezer on the sheet pan until they are firm, and then transfer them into an airtight container. They will last for up to 30 days. When ready to cook, you can go straight from the freezer into the boiling water.

Lemon Chèvre Cream

In a saucepan on medium heat, cook the butter and grapeseed oil until the butter melts. Add the shallots and sauté until soft and translucent. Add the sherry and vegetable stock and stir until well combined. Reduce by half then turn heat to low. Whisk in the chèvre until smooth and let sauce simmer for about 5 minutes. Finish with fresh lemon juice and a little salt and white pepper to taste. Meanwhile, dice the small red and yellow beets into small squares. Set aside.

In a large pot boil water with a generous amount of salt. Gently place the gnocchi into the water and cook for about 3-5 minutes. Do not stir or they will break. Once they float to the top, carefully remove them with a slotted spoon and place them into a bowl until you are ready to plate.

Place some of the chèvre cream into the bottom of each of your individual bowls. Gently place a portion of the gnocchi in the center of the sauce. Garnish with a few pieces of the yellow and red beet, and top with the shaved fennel and a few candied walnuts.

ADAM KREISEL "Restaurants can't contain Adam Kreisel, and kitchens can't get rid of him. He's a one-of-a-kind, Boston born, skiing hippy of sorts…" according to food writers Becky and Josh Rosenthal. Trained in San Francisco, Adam has spent most of his 20-year career in Utah where he has led, innovated, trained and inspired anybody lucky enough to know him. He ran the restaurants at Sundance Resort, cooked for the James Beard Foundation during the Olympics, and opened restaurants such as the Globe Café / by Moonlight awarded Best SLC, Editor's Choice and Reader's Choice. Joining the faculty of Park City Culinary Institute in 2014, Adam teaches how to braise, work with shellfish, make delicious soups and custards, make salmon gravlax, and this beautiful recipe for a fun twist on gnocchi.

Dry Aged Steak with Chimichurri Sauce

1½ lbs dry aged porterhouse or T-bone steak (1-¾ inch thick steak) brought to room temperature
1 Tbsp kosher salt
fresh ground pepper
2 Tbsp grapeseed oil
3 Tbsp unsalted butter

CHIMICHURRI SAUCE
1 cup extra virgin olive oil
½ cup red wine vinegar
1 Tbsp fish sauce, Red Boat brand preferred
5 large cloves of garlic, chopped and minced
1 small shallot, chopped and minced
1 cup Italian parsley, chopped and minced.

1 Tbsp capers, rinsed and chopped
1 tsp oregano, chopped and minced
½ tsp red pepper flakes
1 tsp kosher salt
1½ tsp sugar

Pre heat oven to 250 degrees.

Salt and pepper the beef and set aside on a baking sheet with a wire rack for 20 minutes.

Insert an in-oven thermometer into the center of thickest part of the beef and place in the oven until the temperature reaches 90 degrees fahrenheit.

Once the temperature reaches 90 degrees fahrenheit take the beef out and let rest for about 15-20 minutes. With a cast iron pan or a stainless steel pan bring up to medium high heat. Add grapeseed oil and sear the steak on each side until nicely browned, about 2 minutes each side. Once the steak is brown, add butter and baste with a spoon a few times.

Once basted, remove the steak and place on a wire rack and cover loosely with aluminum foil and let rest for about 15 minutes.

Once rested, carve the steak by depressing both steaks from each side of the bone. You will have a strip loin and a tenderloin. Once you've separated the steaks from the bone, slice them and rearrange them back on a plate with the bone and serve with the chimichurri sauce.

Chimichurri Sauce

Best made the day before.

In a plastic bowl, with a whisk, mix extra virgin olive oil, red wine vinegar, fish sauce, minced garlic, chopped shallots, parsley, capers and, oregano, red pepper flakes, kosher salt and sugar until well combined.

Cover with plastic wrap and place in the refrigerator for at least 3 hours or preferably overnight.

When ready to serve, mix well, season to taste, and then enjoy!

Great over steak, fish, or seafood.

VIET PHAM grew up in the Bay Area with parents who loved to cook. Though his first restaurant, Forage, was a unique concept, it was well received and won Salt Lake Magazine's Best New Restaurant, and Best Restaurant, and Pham won Best Chef. Pham also won Food & Wine Best New Chef, and their nomination for People's Best New Chef: Southwest. The James Beard Foundation nominated Viet as Semi-Finalist for Best Chef: Southwest in 2011, 2012, and 2013.

Pham has appeared on The Food Network's Extreme Chef, The Next Food Network Star, and NBC's Food Fighters. He defeated Bobby Flay on Iron Chef America, and on Kitchen Inferno. Featured in Bon Appetit, The Wall Street Journal, The NY Times, The San Francisco Chronicle, Reuters, and many other national publications, Viet is now opening a new restaurant, ember + ash, in Salt Lake City, and is a Guest Instructor at Park City Culinary Institute.

park city culinary institute
— and event center —

Chocolate Rochers

DV | D

nuts, almonds	milk chocolate	raisins
dark chocolate	hazelnut	apricots
white chocolate	ginger	

Tempering Chocolate

Chocolate is tempered before being packaged for consumers. Melting the chocolate is what makes it go out of temper. Chocolate must be tempered again before using in applications such as candy making. This will restore the original sheen and texture.

A digital instant-read thermometer is necessary to monitor the temperature of the chocolate as you melt and cool the chocolate.

To temper chocolate melt ¾ of the chocolate over a double boiler, stirring often. Reserve the remaining ¼ to use later for cooling.

Bring the chocolate to its melting temperature (120 degrees F for dark chocolate, 115 degrees F for milk or white chocolate).

Next bring the chocolate to its cooling temperature by adding the reserved ¼ of the chocolate and stirring until it is melted (85 degrees for dark, 80 degrees for milk or white chocolate). If the chocolate is still too warm, continue to stir until the air helps it reach the cooling temperature.

Carefully bring the chocolate into its working range (87-91 degrees F for dark chocolate, 84-87 degrees for milk or white chocolate). Do this by reheating over a double boiler for no more than 2 or 3 seconds at a time, stirring, and checking the temperature. Re-heat periodically as you work in order to maintain the working temperature. Do not allow the chocolate to fall out-side of the working range. If this should happen, the chocolate must be tempered again.

Rochers

Toast nuts in a 350 degree oven for 5-10 minutes, stirring occasionally, until the nuts are lightly browned and give off a fragrant aroma. Set aside and allow to cool completely before proceeding. Mix the nuts with your choice of dried fruit in a mixing bowl.

Temper Your Chocolate

You will need to work quickly, as the chocolate will start to harden. Working in small batches in a smaller bowl, add tempered chocolate to coat a handful of nuts and fruit, and then working very quickly with two spoons, place a bite-size mound on a parchment-lined sheet pan. Using the two spoons, pull the mixture up to give it some height. Continue to make small mounds leaving a little bit of space between them on the sheet pan.

The chocolate will cool as you work. To maintain the working range, re-warm periodically as directed in the Chocolate Tempering guidelines.

Precaution: If the temperature of the chocolate rises above or falls below the working range, it must be re-tempered.

REBECCA MILLICAN has over 25 years' experience in baking and pastry, and joins Park City Culinary Institute from the Institute of Culinary Education in New York. A Utah native, Rebecca was the chocolatier at Amano Artisan Chocolate, and led the pastry team at Culinary Crafts. Rebecca is now the Executive Pastry Chef at la Caille, and has appeared in several episodes of Food Network Challenge and most recently, in Season 4, of Food Network's Halloween Wars. Rebecca joined the faculty of Park City Culinary Institute in 2015.

ROCHER ("rock"), which refers to the appearance of these fruit and nut clusters. Rebecca's favorite combinations include almonds and raisins in white chocolate, almonds and apricots in milk chocolate, and hazelnut and ginger in dark chocolate.

TIP FROM VIET *These chocolates are displayed on a piece of wood from our fireplace. You can forage at home for leaves from a nearby tree, pine needles, and other natural elements to make your presentation unique and memorable.*

park city culinary institute
— and event center —

"Cocchi Spritz" Cocktail

(DV) | (D)

1 oz Charbay blood orange vodka
1 oz Aperol

1 oz Cocchi Americano (can substitute Lillet
Blanc but defeats the purpose)

2 oz Prosecco

Someplace where martinis, negronis and Aperol spritz collide, Chef and Sommelier Greg Neville presents the "Cocchi Spritz"

Mix Charbay blood orange vodka, Aperol and Cocchi Americano with ice. Shake well.
Pour into classic coupe champagne or martini glass with sugared rim.
Add prosecco. Garnish with orange twist.

Lobster Carpaccio, con't from page 96 For lobster shell garnish, the head shell should pull free from remaining legs and body. Again using scissors, cut the head in 2 length wise. Trim head to desired size keeping the antennae intact. Rinse off any unwanted residue and reserve for plating.

Carrot, Radish and Ginger Puree
Heat butter in sauce pan under medium to high heat. Add carrot, radish, ginger and garlic. Stir until garlic begins to lightly brown. Add thyme and nutmeg. Quickly add white wine. Briefly stir together. Add stock, reduce heat and let simmer for 10 minutes, until carrots are soft. Place mixture into blender and puree until smooth. Taste for salt and pepper. Add a splash of cream, drizzle of olive oil or pat of butter to reach desired consistency. Chill and reserve for plating.

Vanilla Bean Extra Virgin Olive Oil
Place scraped vanilla bean seeds and pod and all other ingredients into small squeeze bottle. Shake well. Set aside. May be made the morning of or kept refrigerated for 2 – 3 days.

Lobster Tapenade
Place all ingredients in mixing bowl. Taste for salt, pepper, lemon and olive oil. Reserve.

Assembly
Spread carrot puree on plate with large soup spoon. Slice lobster tail into 10 slices, 5 for each plate. Layer lobster slices on top of puree. Spoon a dollop of lobster tapenade onto one end of the plate. Place a few orange and grapefruit sections onto plate. Drizzle vanilla bean olive oil over lobster slices. Add scallions, thyme leaves, edible flowers and lobster shell for garnish. Enjoy!!

POWDER

P☼WDER

POWDER AT CANYONS VILLAGE

CV

RYKER BROWN

Impeccable service and gracious style await each arrival at Powder. Located within the Waldorf Astoria Park City, and nestled among the pristine Wasatch Mountains, this Forbes Four-Star restaurant captures the essence of the mountains with seasonal menus focused on locally sourced products and foraged ingredients.

Established in December of 2011, and led by Executive Chef Ryker Brown, Powder offers guests a dining experience as grand as the surrounding mountains. With slopeside access to the largest ski resort in the United States, Park City Mountain Resort, and complimentary valet parking, guests find an easy dining indulgence for their mountain retreat. The experience is convivial and relaxed with a lounge-esque indoor dining area and a more intimate private dining space next to the wine bar with larger table seating. Powder offers additional outdoor seasonal dining with views of the pool and scenic courtyard. During the winter season, Powder is the ideal location to gather for après ski beverages with a full service bar and cozy outdoor fire pits. With live music during the weekend dinner hours, guests relish in a dining experience unlike any other in Canyons Village.

Open for breakfast, lunch, après, and dinner, guests savor a modern mountain menu driven by the seasons and inspired by the finest local ingredients. Powder's modern interpretation focuses on direct flavor and straightforward presentation. Technique and imagination balanced with fresh, contemporary cuisine and the heartiness of the bountiful mountains of Utah create an exceptional dining experience. The restaurant offers an unparalleled wine and spirits program, including handcrafted cocktails and an extensive list of wines from around the world.

Chef Brown's personal love for jalapeños is shown in several of his dishes including the Oysters with Hogwash recipe. The Hogwash is his style of a Mignonette sauce, which is a traditional vinegar based sauce to which he adds jalapeño and cilantro. Powder recommends a perfect wine pairing of a New Zealand Sauvignon Blanc, due to its grapefruit notes.

While his culinary career began in California, Brown has spent most of his career working in mountain resort destinations including Big Sky Resort (as the Executive Sous Chef) and as the Executive Sous for the Yellowstone Club at Rainbow Lodge.

In 2008, he accepted the Executive Chef position at Promontory Ranch Club, and worked his way to Sundance Mountain Resort as the Resort Executive Chef from 2012 to 2014.

Ryker combines traditional techniques, with new methods, such as sous-vide and basted meats.

His focus on natural ingredients has enhanced Powder's local product use, such as Heber Valley Cheese and Creminelli cured meats for charcuteries, and the use of herbs and honey from our backyard garden and beehive.

PG106   PG107

POWDER

West Coast Oysters Hogwash

12 Shigoku oyster or any west coast oyster,
1 lime, juiced
4 Tbsp rice wine vinegar

1 bunch cilantro, chopped
½ jalapeno, diced, with seeds
3 Tbsp shallots, diced

Oysters

Rinse oysters under cold, running water. Place oyster flat-side up on hard surface, and grip with kitchen towel, leaving hinged end exposed.

Put tip of oyster knife between top and bottom shells, next to the hinge. Press inward, while twisting and wiggling your knife, until open. Keep oyster level to retain natural oyster juices inside the deep, bottom shell.

Wipe knife of debris, and pry open shell.

Run oyster knife along the top of upper shell to cut the oysters' muscle. Cut along lower shell, and free oyster.

Prepare

Combine lime juice, rice wine vinegar, chopped cilantro, diced jalapeno, diced shallots.

Mix well. Mixture should be thick like relish.

In a serving bowl, fill ¾ way full of crushed ice.

Arrange oysters on ice.

Place ½ Tablespoon Hogwash on each oyster.

POWDER

Pan Seared Utah Trout with Braised Cabbage, Mussels and Beets

TROUT
2 6 oz trout filets
sprigs thyme
salt & pepper to taste
1 Granny Smith, julienne
2 Tbsp canola oil

BRAISED CABBAGE
1 head cabbage, purple, julienned
1 cup red wine vinegar
½ cup agave nectar
salt & pepper

BEETS & MUSSELS
1 lbs baby yellow beets
5 sprigs fresh thyme
Salt & pepper
½ lbs mussels
3 Tbsp canola oil
1 Tbsp butter

Trout
Heat canola oil in sautée pan over high heat.
Season trout filets with salt and pepper.
Lay trout skin side down and cook until golden brown and the skin is crispy.
Flip trout over and add butter and thyme sprigs. Baste.

Braised Cabbage
In a sautée pan on medium heat, add 1 tablespoon canola oil
Saute cabbage for 5 minutes
Add remaining ingredients and cook on low heat for 1 hour

Mussels and Beets
Preheat oven to 250 degrees.
Place beets in a 9 x 13 pan and drizzle 2 tablespoon canola oil, salt, pepper and thyme. Cover with foil.
Place beets in oven and roast for 3 hours or until tender.
Allow beets to cool and peel them using a cloth to wipe and remove the skin.
Heat a sautée pan on medium high heat and add 1 tablespoon canola oil and 1 tablespoon butter.
Add beets and mussels and cook until mussels open.

Remove from heat and remove the meat of the mussels and discard the shell. Salt and pepper to taste.

Julienne 1 Granny Smith apple.
On a clean plate, place beets, mussels and cabbage in center.
Lay trout filets on top.
Garnish with apples.

Season to taste.

RED TAIL GRILL
at canyons village

RED TAIL GRILL
AT CANYONS VILLAGE

CV

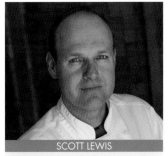

SCOTT LEWIS

Red Tail Grill offers progressive tap house fare along-side amazing views in the mountains. Located within the Grand Summit Hotel on the Ski Beach in Canyons Village, Red Tail Grill features an innovative menu served in a rustic setting. With its outdoor deck, Red Tail Grill is a perfect gathering spot for family-friendly dining.

Ingredients are sourced from local, sustainable vendors including Wasatch Meats, Stone Ground Bakery, and Gold Creek Farm. You might start your meal with Smoked Utah Trout Crostini or Chili Rubbed Wings. For an entree, choose from the Bone-In Pork Chop, or expand your palette with the Tap House chicken. Then move on to the hefty Cowboy burger, or bratwurst cooked in beer. You may enjoy your evening meal so much, that you'll come back for breakfast before your ski day, then back again for lunch for the Goat Cheese Caprese Sandwich,or Smoked Brisket.

Park City Mountain Resort and Canyons Resort combined in the summer of 2015-2016 to create the largest single ski and snowboard resort in the United States.

The new, 8 passenger Quicksilver Gondola connection, along with the new Miners Camp Restaurant, King Con Express six-pack and Motherlode Express quad made up just some of the resort improvements totaling over $50 million for the 2015-16 season.

With over 7,300 acres, 300+ trails, 41 lifts, six terrain parks, one super pipe and one mini pipe, plus many diverse ski-in/ski-out and village adjacent lodging properties, Park City is an easily accessible, world-class mountain destination located in an authentic and historic western town.

Scott Lewis is the Senior Executive Chef at the Grand Summit Hotel and Village-Chef. A husband and father, Chef Lewis is dedicated to the culinary riches of great food, fresh ideas and renewed ingredients since he first learned how to make tamales and scratch sauces at the age of eight.

With more than twenty years in the business, Lewis has cooked in New Zealand, Australia, Park City and Napa Valley. He apprenticed under Chef de Cuisine to CMC Henry Sing Cheng for sixteen years and earned glowing reviews in the New York Times and the coveted American Academy of Hospitality Sciences Five Star Diamond Award. He is passionate about preserving and promoting local ingredients and continuing to provide guests with extraordinary dining experiences.

PG112   PG113   PG114   PG115   PG116

French Onion Dip

8 Spanish onions, finely diced and caramelized
3 Tbls butter
2 Tbls olive oil
8 cups sour cream
2 cups buttermilk
2 cups mayonaisse
½ cup scallions
3 Tbsp granulated garlic

3 Tbsp granulated onion
1 Tbsp honey
½ cup Worcestershire sauce
1 Tbsp Tabasco
Kosher salt and fresh black pepper
fresh chives, minced
homemade potato chips
vegetable crudites

In a large skillet heat oil and butter in a large skillet. Add onions and salt and pepper to taste. Stirring constantly, cook onions until the onions soften. Approximately 5 minutes.

In large mixing bowl combine onions, sour cream, buttermilk, mayonaisse, scallions, granulated garlic, granulated onion, honey, worcestershire sauce, Tabasco™, kosher salt and fresh black pepper to taste.

Add fresh chives for a bonus earthy onion flavor.

Blend thoroughly to the desired consistency.

Enjoy with homemade potato chips or as a crudité dipping sauce.

Our Onion dip is a great all season favorite in Park City, skiers and golfers alike.

Roasted Beet Hummus

2 small (3-ounce) beets
6 cups garbanzo beans, rinsed and drained
⅓ cup tahini
2 Tbsp roasted garlic
¼ cup lemon juice
¼ tsp fine sea salt
1 Tbsp extra virgin olive oil
pinch cayenne pepper

ROASTED GARLIC
garlic bulb of choice
1 Tbsp olive oil
salt and pepper to taste

Pre heat oven to 450 degrees. Scrub beets, sprinkle with salt and pepper and lightly coat with the olive oil..
Roast in aluminum foil or covered pan until soft and aromatic. Cool beets, peel and set aside.
In food processor combine garbanzo beans, tahini, roasted garlic, lemon juice and sea salt, blend until smooth and creamy.
Add beets and continue to blend until a beautiful purple color.
Salt and pepper to taste.

Roasted Garlic
Preheat oven to 425 degrees.
Cut off the top of the garlic so you have a space to pour in your olive oil. Drizzle the olive oil into the garlic slots until filled and running down the sides of the garlic bulb.
Seal garlic bulb in aluminum foil and cook on a baking sheet for 30-35 minutes, until garlic is tender and fragrant.
Remove from the oven and let cool.
Peel off the outside of the bulb and one by one squeeze out each garlic clove.

Smoked Utah Trout Crostini

½ cup smoked Utah trout
½ tsp bloomed (fried) capers
1 sprig fresh dill
1 baguette, sliced
lemon oil, or
    herb infused oil
Olive Oil
Salt and pepper

TROUT MOUSSE
1 lbs cream cheese
3 Tbsp goat cheese
1 Tbsp minced garlic
1 Tbsp lemon juice
1 Tbsp Tabasco
½ cup smoked trout
2 Tbsp chopped parsley
1 tsp granulated garlic
1 tsp granulated onion
1 tsp white pepper
2 Tbsp fresh chives, chopped
sea salt to taste

PEPPERADE
2 cups red wine vinegar
¾ cups white sugar
2½ roasted red bell peppers, minced
¾ tsp fresh ground black pepper

SLURRY
cornstarch
water

Trout Mousse
In a medium saucepan combine cream cheese, goat cheese, minced garlic, lemon juice, Tabasco, ½ cup smoked trout, granulated garlic, granulated onion, and white pepper and bring to a boil.
Thicken with slurry, equal parts water and cornstarch, mixed until slightly thicker than jelly.
Transfer all to a food processor.
Add fresh chive and parsley and blend all ingredients in food processor until smooth and silky. Add Sea Salt if desired.

Pepperade
Combine the vinegar, sugar, minced red peppers and black pepper in a medium saucepan. Bring to a boil, reduce heat and simmer very gently until mixture has broken down and thickened. Remove from heat and cool.

Assembly
Brush baguette slices with olive oil and season lightly with salt and pepper. Grill or toast under broiler.
Top each of the crostini with some of the mousse and then a dollop of the pepperade.
Add lemon or herb infused oil of your choice to further enhance your dining experience.
For best results find local smoked trout at specialty markets.

Serves 4

CROSTINI In Italian, crostino means "little toast", and usually consists of a small slice of toasted bread with topping of cheeses, meats, and vegetables, brushed with olive oil, herbs, or sauces. It's thought that they date back to medieval times when Italians ate their meals on bread instead of costly ceramic plates.

Ale Battered Fish and Chips

6 9 oz fresh cod, per serving
4 6 oz English chips or French fries
¼ lemon
2 oz tartar sauce
3 oz beer batter
Canola oil for deep fry

BEER BATTER
2 cup beer or ale
1 cups flour
2 Tbsp kosher salt
1 Tbsp Old Bay seasoning
1 Tbsp black pepper
2 tsp ground mustard

TARTAR SAUCE
2 cups mayonnaise
⅛ cup sweet pickled relish
⅛ tsp lemon juice
⅛ tsp pepperoncini juice
⅛ cup fresh dill
¼ tsp Tabasco
salt and fresh ground pepper
sriracha

Beer Batter
This batter will give you a crispy, flakey crust.
Combine one part flour to two parts beer or ale.
Combine flour, Kosher salt, Old Bay seasoning, black pepper, and ground mustard.
Combine the flour mixture and the beer.
Gently dredge fresh cod filet in beer batter allowing for excess batter to drip free from fish and drop slowly into submerged fry basket.
Allow to brown lightly on one side and flip with fryer safe utensil of choice.

Continue frying until fish is evenly golden brown and floating, for about 4 minutes.
Serve and enjoy with Tartar sauce and fresh lemon.

Tartar Sauce
In a medium mixing bowl whisk mayonnaise, sweet pickled relish, pepperoncini juice, fresh dill, Tabasco sauce, and salt and fresh ground pepper to taste.
Add sriracha to the tartar sauce for an extra kick.

Grilled Salmon with Shaved Asparagus

7 oz fresh Atlantic salmon filet, per serving
7 asparagus spears
4 oz Utah corn succotash
2 oz sherry vinaigrette

UTAH CORN SUCCOTASH
1 small red onion, chopped
2 garlic cloves, minced
4 ears Utah corn, kernels cut off and
   cobs discarded
1 large fresh jalapeno chile, seeded and finely
   chopped
3oz zucchini, medium dice
3oz yellow squash, medium dice
3oz green beans, cleaned and blanched
¾ lbs cherry tomatoes (1 pint), halved
2 Tbsp sherry vinaigrette
salt and freshly ground black pepper

SHERRY VINAIGRETTE
¼ cup garlic cloves
¼ cup whole peeled shallot
¼ cup lemon juice
½ cup Guldens brown mustard
2 Tbsp whole grain mustard
½ cup honey
½ lb brown sugar
2 cup sherry
2 cup apple cider vinegar
2 Tbsp granulated onion
1 Tbsp white pepper
2 Tbsp salt
2½ qts oil blend

Grilled Salmon
Lightly oil, salt and pepper and grill to desired temperature, until the salmon is irridescent in color and not dry.
Layers of the fish should be peel away easily with fork.

Shaved Asparagus
With potato peeler, shave asparagus raw into long thin leaf like strands. Store in ice cold water, covered until time to serve.
To serve, drain, dry, and add to pre-heated saute pan with 1 tablespoon oil. Flash fry 30 seconds, add salt and pepper and remove from heat. Serves as garnish on top of Salmon.

Utah Corn Succotash
Heat sauté pan with 1 tablespoon of olive oil and add onion, jalapeno and corn and cook for 45 seconds. Add squash, zucchini and green beans. Saute together for 2 minutes and finish with cherry tomatoes, sherry vinaigrette and salt and pepper. Be careful not to overcook as this will mute your beautiful fresh colors.
Serve beneath the salmon as a wonderful accompaniment of vegetables and starch.

Sherry Vinaigrette
In a blender, or immersion hand blender, emulsify all ingredients.
Slowly add in oil blend until smooth and creamy. Drizzle on or around Salmon to finish dish.

For a summertime entré try making a larger batch of the succotash with any vegetable that you like.

RIVERHORSE
ON MAIN
Est. 1987

RIVERHORSE ON MAIN

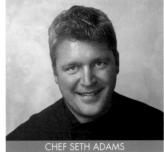

CHEF SETH ADAMS

Riverhorse on Main was the first Mobil and Forbes 4 Star restaurant in Utah - an honor the restaurant has received for 16 consecutive years - as well as the AAA 4-Diamond award and the distinguished DiRoNa Award.

Signature Riverhorse dishes like its world-famous macadamia-encrusted halibut and wild game trio keep visitors and locals coming back. By using only the freshest of ingredients and sourcing locally as much as possible, Chef Adams has created a style that is a benchmark for the New American cuisine movement in Utah.

In 2011 Missouri businessman Dave Spence and his wife, Suzie, bought Riverhorse on Main, with Seth and his wife, Casey, as partners. With the collective talent of four new owners, Riverhorse on Main launched into new heights. Along with Chef Adams skill, his wife Casey, a talented interior designer, transformed the Riverhorse into a breathtaking place. With the Spence's business acumen and boundless energy, it's been a very successful partnership.

The food at Riverhorse on Main is an eclectic mix of New American cuisine, featuring time-honored favorites and seasonal masterpieces. Menu classics include the Utah Red Trout with Pistachio crust, a Wild Game Trio with Port Wine Reduction and Huckleberry Compote, and an Overnight Braised Buffalo Short Rib that guests rave about as one of their best meals ever. A table at Riverhorse is certain to include items that are locally sourced, as well as rare and hard-to-obtain surprises. Diners raved, "Extraordinary dining experience in Park City", "Must dine-for foodie families", "Sculpted cuisine".

It's become a destination all of its own. Guests from all over the world vie for a coveted table at Riverhorse during the ski season, and it has become the centerpiece for destination weddings and business retreats. The unique combination of stunning flexible space, is evident every January when the restaurant becomes the place to "see and be seen," during Sundance Film Festival. It's an upscale destination serving fine wines and American fare, with live music, in an elegant setting.

The most significant event in the Riverhorse story is the arrival of Chef Seth Adams in 2001. He bacame the executive chef in 2004.

With a respect for tradition and a flare for innovation, Chef Adams put Riverhorse on the map. Considered one of the top young chefs in America, his vision, drive, and passion took Riverhorse, by then a well-established venue, to the next level.

Building on signature Riverhorse dishes like its world famous macadamia crusted halibut and wild game trio, chef Adams has developed a menu with extraordinary depth and character.

Seth has boyish good looks and charm, but underneath it all is a culinary genius that has expoded on the Park City restaurant scene.

PG122 PG123 PG124 PG125 PG126

Poached Pear & Burrata Salad with Local Honey and Cream Cheese Stuffed Dates

1 lb Burrata cheese, drained
10 oz micro greens

POACHED PEARS
4 Bartlett pears, peeled and cored
½ cup white wine
4 cups water
2 cups sugar

BALSAMIC VINAIGRETTE
½ cup balsamic vinegar
1½ cups olive oil
1 Tbsp Dijon mustard
½ tsp minced garlic
salt and pepper to taste
2 tsp fresh thyme, chopped

STUFFED DATES
dried dates, as needed
1 cup cream cheese, softened
2 Tbsp raw Utah honey
½ Tbsp pepper

MACERATED FIGS
1 cup dried figs, halved
1 cup balsamic vinegar

In a sauce pan combine the water, sugar and white wine. Peel and core pears and add and bring to a boil; reduce heat and simmer for 15-20 minutes until pears are tender. Remove from heat and let cool.

Vinaigrette
In a blender, combine balsamic vinegar, mustard, garlic, thyme, salt and pepper. Slowly blend in olive oil.

Stuffed Dates
Mix together softened cream cheese, honey and pepper. Place mixture into piping bag and fill dates.

Macerated Figs
Combine figs with balsamic vinegar and macerate for 2 hours

Assembly
Place poached pears on plate, topped with Burrata cheese, cut in half, micro greens, drizzled with balsamic vinaigrette, garnish with macerated figs.

MACERATE Just as you would marinate vegetables, fruit can be marinated. Macerate fresh or dried fruit by splashing or soaking your fruit in a flavored liqueur, vinegar or syrup over night or for just a few hours. By soaking the fruit it takes on the liquids and its seasonings. It also plumps up and softens the fruit.

Roasted Sweet Corn and Vegetable Gazpacho

6 ears fresh sweet corn
salt & pepper
olive oil
3 red bell pepper, roasted and diced
3 english cucumber, seeded and diced
1 jalapeno, seeded and diced

1 sweet onion, diced
1 red onion, diced
3 limes, juiced
1½ cup tomato paste
4 qt vegetable stock
4 tsp cumin

4 tsp chili powder
¼ Tbsp cayenne powder
1 tsp salt
½ cup Italian parsley, chopped
½ cup cilantro, chopped

Preheat grill.
Brush corn and bell peppers with oil, salt and pepper. Grill corn until cooked and bell peppers roasted. Cool and cut corn from husk. Peel, seed and dice red bell peppers.
Place the corn and diced red peppers in a large bowl.
Dice cucumber, jalapeno, sweet onion and red onion, add to corn and red peppers.
Mix together the cumin, chili powder, cayene powder, salt, chopped parsley and chopped cilantro and add to vegetables.
Add tomato paste, vegetable stock and lime juice.
Season to taste and refrigerate.

Pistachio Crusted Utah Red Trout with
Pomegranate Fennel Salsa and Lemon Beurre Blanc

4 6 oz trout filets
buttermilk, as needed
olive oil, as needed

BREADING
1 cup pistachio nuts, ground
1 cup Panko bread crumbs
1 Tbsp salt
½ Tbsp pepper

POMEGRANATE FENNEL SALSA
1 cup pomegranate seeds
1 cup fennel, minced
1 cup rice wine vinegar
½ cup extra virgin olive oil
3 Tbsp honey
1 bunch cilantro, chopped
1 tsp salt
½ tsp pepper

LEMON BEURRE BLANC
¼ cup shallots, chopped
1 oz olive oil
½ cup lemon juice
1 lb butter, unsalted, softened
    at room temperature
salt, to taste
white pepper
cayenne pepper

Preheat oven to 425 Degrees
In a food processor, blend the pistachio nuts until it resembles coarse corn meal. Then add the Panko bread crumbs, salt and pepper. Set Aside.
Place the trout filets in the buttermilk and then crust with breading on both sides.

Pomegranate Fennerl Salsa
Mix the pomegranate seeds, fennel, rice wine vinegar, olive oil, honey, cilantro and salt and pepper together and chill.

Lemon Beurre Blanc
In a sauce pan heat the olive oil until almost smoking, add the chopped shallots and sauté for 1 minute stirring constantly not letting them get brown. Then add the lemon juice and reduce heat. Simmer the lemon juice until it is almost dry. Remove from heat.
Soften the butter to room remperature and divide into 6 equal portions. Using a wisk, slowly wisk the softened butter one portion at a time into the oil, shallot mixture. Making sure to keep the sauce at the same temperature. Do not boil.
Season the mixture with salt, white pepper and cayenne to taste. Strain the sauce through a double mesh.

In a sauté pan, heat some oil until almost smoking. Place the trout in the olive oil flesh side down, sear until brown, flip the fish and finish in the pre-heated oven for about 3 – 4 minutes Top with lemon sauce and pomegranate salsa. Serve with rice and fresh vegetables

Macadamia Nut Crusted Alaskan Halibut with Lemon Beurre Blanc

4 6 oz portions of fresh Alaskan halibut

BREADING
1 2 lb loaf of sourdough bread, ground
1 small bunch Italian parsley, chopped
½ cup macadamia nuts, chopped
¾ cup olive oil
1 Tbsp salt
½ Tbsp pepper

LEMON BEURRE BLANC
¼ cup shallots, chopped
1 oz olive oil
½ cup Lemon juice
1lb butter, unsalted- softened
   at room temperature
salt and white pepper to taste
cayenne pepper to taste

MANGO CHUTNEY
2 ripe mangoes
1 tsp chili garlic sauce
   (available at Asian market)
½ bunch Italian parsley, chopped

Preheat oven to 425 degrees.
In a food processor, pulse the bread to the consistency of coarse corn meal. Then pulse the macadamia nut to the same consistency. Add the chopped parsley, oil, salt and pepper.

Lemon Beurre Blanc Sauce

In a sauce pan, heat the olive oil until almost smoking. Add the chopped shallots and sauté for 1 minute stirring constantly not letting them get brown. Then add the lemon juice and reduce heat. Simmer the lemon juice until it is almost dry. Remove from heat.
Soften the butter to room remperature and divide into 6 equal portions. Using a wisk, slowly wisk the softened butter one portion at a time into the oil, shallot mixture. Make sure to keep the sauce at the same temperature. Do not boil.
Season the mixture with salt, white pepper and cayenne to taste. Strain the sauce through a double mesh.

Mango Chutney

Peel and seed the mangoes. Medium dice 1 mango and puree the other mango in food processor. Mix together with chopped parsley and chili garlic sauce.

Assembly

Place the halibut on an oiled oven proof platter. Top the fish with the bread mixture and bake in oven for 8- 10 minutes. Top with lemon beurre blanc and serve with the mango chutney, fresh seasonal vegetables and mashed potatoes.

Serves 4

Seared Beef Tenderloin with Spiced Red Wine Brown Butter Jus with Parsnip Purée

1 whole tenderloin, or Wagyu beef
salt and freshly ground black pepper

SPICED RED WINE BROWN BUTTER JUS
½ chili arbol, broken
1½ tsp coriander, whole seed
¼ tsp cumin, whole seed
¼ tsp fenugreek

⅛ tsp brown mustard, whole seed
1 pod black cardamom, whole pod,
   lightly crushed
2 whole cloves
½ whole star anise
1 yellow onion, sliced
1 carrot, sliced
½ cup celery rood, sliced

1 parsnip, sliced
2 bottles of red wine
5 sprigs thyme
1 bunch parsley
1 bay leaf
¼ cup butter, browned
butter, as need

Beef Tenderloin
Bring beef tenderloin to room temperature. Season liberally with salt and black pepper. Sear on all sides and roast to medium rare.

Spiced Red Wine Brown Butter Jus
Lightly toast the chili arbol, coriander seeds, cumin seeds, fenugreek, brown mustard seeds, lightly crushed black cardamon pods, whole cloves and whole star anise. Put aside.

Caramelize yellow onions, carrots, celery root and parsnip.
Add the wine and bring to a boil. Simmer for 45 minutes.
In a separate bowl add the parsley, thyme and bay leaf and simmer for another 45 minutes.
Strain the vegetables and discard them. Add the spice mixture to the vegetable liquid. Simmer for 30 minutes. Strain again, return to saucepan; and reduce the sauce to desired consistency. Season with salt and pepper to taste.

Serve with a parsnip purée.
Serves 20

SAMMY'S BISTRO

Ⓟ

When you dine at Sammy's Bistro, all of Sammy's extensive knowledge of Italian, French, and Asian cuisine shines through. Sammy's Bistro has diverse items like the Thai Chicken Lettuce Wraps, Mahi Mahi Tacos with Mango Salsa, Grilled Romaine Wedge, the "Chivito Club" sandwich, and Savory Chicken Bowl with Rice.

Sammy's Bistro opened its doors on January 17th, 2010. Sammy was inspired on the Farmer's Market circuit, and cooking on the street for locals every weekend. "Sammy's Texas BBQ Shrimp" was one of the first food vendors at the Park Silly Sunday Market on Main Street in Park City in 2006. He sold his now famous Bacon Wrapped Shrimp with Jalapenos, Asian Coleslaw, and Frozen Lemonade to the hot and hungry locals on Main Street. After being wildly successful for 5 years doing the circuit, Sammy moved from the carnival atmosphere on the street to a brick and mortar establishment, creating Sammy's Bistro on Bonanza Drive.

Sammy incorporated recipes from his travels abroad and from his roots working at Mileti's and Shabu to create an eclectic and unique menu that locals swear by and tourists are thrilled to stumble upon. "Eat here once and you are hooked" Sammy claims. "The flavor and quality of the food is the backbone of the restaurant." Although humble in origins, Sammy's Bistro has been featured on Diners Drive-ins & Dives, and has established itself as an anchor in the Park City culinary world.

Featuring a beautiful 25-foot maple bar, 4 flatscreen T.V.'s and a fun staff, Sammy's Bistro is casual, current, and hip. The restaurant is usually fast paced and has a palpable energy that makes it a fun place to eat. You will not be surprised to see some of the best winter athletes sitting next to you, enjoying a jalapeno cream ale and fish tacos. World champion alpine skier Ted Ligety, X-Games champion Simon Dumont, andOlympic Champion Joe Pack are all regulars at Sammy's Bistro. Don't let the funky strip mall fool you; Sammy's Bistro is a legitimate contender in the heavyweight battle of the Park City restaurant scene. Sammy says, "Thank you!"

Samuel Harris is the owner and operator of Sammy's Bistro. He is a 1994 graduate of Park City High School, and has lived in Park City since he was 4 years old.

Sammy is a true ski bum at heart, having competed in mogul and big mountain extreme skiing contests during the day, and cooking at night to support his skiing habit.

Harris has worked in a number of local restaurants, from Mileti's (Italian), The Goldener Hirsch (Alpine Cuisine), Chenez (classical French), and Shabu (Japanese fusion), working under master chefs such as Valter Nassi, Jean Louis Montecot, Gregg Grass, and Bob Valaika.

Sammy worked his way to the top the old school way: 20 years of working hard, and learning from the best.

PG132 · PG133 · PG134 · PG135 · PG136

Grilled Romaine Wedge

½ head romaine lettuce,
   cut lengthwise into 2 quarters
¼ olive oil
salt and pepper
2 Tbsp diced tomatoes
2 Tbsp cooked bacon, crushed

ONION HAY
onion
buttermilk
flour
vegetable oil

FOUR CHEESE DRESSING:
½ cup Fontina, shredded
½ cup Gruyere, shredded
½ cup Parmesan, shredded
½ cup Gorgonzola, shredded
2 cups heavy cream
2 Tbsp shallots
1 cup Franzia chablis wine

Coat the romaine heads with olive oil, salt and pepper.
Grill over high heat for 3 minutes per side, until blackened on edges and warm in middle.
Top with tomatoes and bacon bits.
Top with warm four cheese dressing.
Garnish on top with the fried onion rings.

Onion Hay
Heat vegegable oil in a large frying pan over medium heat.
Slice onion into rings. Select 4 rings.
Place buttermilk in a bowl large enough to soak each ring, then coat thoroughly in flour.
Deep fry turning with tongs, and cook both sides until crispy.

4 Cheese Dressing
Boil wine, cream, and shallots.
Add Fontina, Gruyere, Parmesan, and Gorgonzola cheese, stirring constantly at medium temperature until fully melted and smooth.

Savory Chicken Bowl with Rice

2 lbs boneless, skinless chicken thighs
¼ cup light olive oil
2 cups dry jasmine rice
2 poblano peppers, diced
2½ cups water
1 yellow onion, diced
3 fresh garlic cloves, minced
½ Tbsp yellow curry powder
½ Tbsp paprika

½ Tbsp cumin
½ Tbsp onion powder
½ Tbsp garam masala curry powder
Water
1 bunch cilantro, shredded, for garnish
1 avocado, sliced, for garnish
Fried tortilla strips (for garnish), tossed with taco seasoning and cumin

TOMATILLO AIOLI
10 tomatillos
2 bunches cilantro
⅕ cup buttermilk
2 limes, juiced
2 Tbsp taco seasoning
2 cups mayonnaise
1 Tbsp taco seasoning
½ fresh jalapeno

In a large stock pot, sauté onions and peppers in olive oil over med high heat for 5 minutes.

Add chicken, garlic, and all spices and sautee for another 8 minutes over medium heat until chicken starts to brown. Make sure that the garlic doesn't burn and the chicken is fully coated in the spice mixture.

Add water until it is just covering the chicken. Turn to low heat and simmer for 4 hours, until the chicken is broken down and easily shredded with a fork.

Rice
Rinse rice several times until water is clear.
Strain rice and place rice into rice cooker with 2½ cups of water. Turn on automatic rice cooker until done.

Tomatillo Aioli
In a blender, place tomatillos, cilantro, buttermilk, lime juice, taco seasoning, mayo, taco seasoning, fresh jalapeno and pulse until smooth.

Serve in a 9 oz bowl, with one scoop of cooked rice topped with 6 oz ladle of chicken, and some juice.

Top with a 2 oz. scoop of tomatillo aioli. Garnish with shredded cilantro, tortilla strips, and sliced avocados

Chivito Club Sandwich

1 pork tenderloin
8 inch hoagie rolls from Stoneground Bakery
8 romaine lettuce leaves
1 tomato, sliced
2 slices cooked bacon
1 jumbo egg

SPICY MAYO
1 cup mayonnaise
2 Tbsp sriracha

MARINADE FOR PORK TENDERLOIN
½ cup soy sauce
1 tsp minced ginger
1 tsp minced garlic
½ cup canola oil
1 Tbsp cilantro
¼ cup lemon juice

TOMATILLO AIOLI
5 tomatillos
1 bunches cilantro
¾ cups buttermilk
1 limes, juiced
1 Tbsp taco seasoning
1 cups mayonnaise
¼ fresh jalapeno

In medium sized casserole dish or bowl place soy sauce, minced ginger, minced garlic, canola oil, cilantro and lemon juice. Place pork tenderloin into marinade for 30 minutes.
Remove the tenderloin from marinade and grill on a gas or BBQ grill over medium temperature for 10-12 minutes, until meat thermometer reads 165 degrees in the thickest portion of the pork tenderloin.
Remove from heat and let rest on cutting board while you are preparing the spicy mayo and tomatillo aioli for the sandwich.

Tomatillo Aioli
In a blender, place tomatillos, cilantro, buttermilk, lime juice, taco seasoning, mayonnaise, fresh jalapeno and pulse until smooth.

Spicy Mayo
Mix mayonnaise and sriracha together. Add sriracha for your particular spice level.

Assemble
Fry an egg in non-stick pan until over medium. Place aside. Take the hoagie roll and slice lengthwise. Toast on griddle with melted butter.

Remove from griddle. Put 1 tablespoon of the spicy mayonnaise and 1 tablespoon of the tomatillo aioli on hoagie.
Slice the pork crossways into thin medallions.
Arrange pork on top of sauced bread and top with two slices of cooked bacon.
Top with lettuce, tomato, and fried egg.
Press hoagie together and slice in half.

Served with French fries, potato chips, salad, or Asian coleslaw on page 136.

Mahi Mahi Tacos

P | E

8 oz filet of mahi mahi
¼ cabbage, shredded
2 carrots, shredded
2 Tbsp fresh cilantro, minced
4 6 inch corn Tortillas
¼ cup oil
salt and pepper, pinch
Taco seasoning, pinch
lime wedges for garnish
Cholula hot sauce, to taste

MANGO SALSA
2 cups diced mango
½ cup diced red bell pepper
½ cup diced red onion
½ cup minced cilantro
¼ cup lemon juice
2 Tbsp sugar
salt pepper

TOMATILLO AIOLI
5 tomatillos
1 bunche cilantro
¾ cups buttermilk
1 lime, juiced
1 Tbsp taco seasoning
1 cups mayonnaise
¼ fresh jalapeno

Coat mahi mahi with oil, use as needed to coat, salt and pepper, and taco seasoning. Grill on medium high heat on gas or charcoal BBQ for 5-7 minutes. You want the mahi mahi to flake to the touch.
Place mahi mahi in mixing bowl and set aside.
Warm the corn tortillas on griddle or skillet over medium heat with a touch of oil. Warm throughout but not too crispy.
Mix shredded cabbage and shredded carrots to create a coleslaw mix; you will need about 1 cup for four tacos.

Mango Salsa
In a large bowl, mix diced mango, diced red bell pepper, diced red onion, minced cilantro, lemon juice, sugar and salt pepper to taste.
Serve at room temperature.

Tomatillo Aioli
In a blender, place tomatillos, cilantro, buttermilk, lime juice, taco seasoning, mayonnaise, fresh jalapeno and pulse until smooth.

Assemble
Place mahi mahi in middle of each tortilla and top with coleslaw mix (1/4 cup per taco), 1 Tbsp tomatillo aioli, 1 Tbsp mango salsa, and a pinch of fresh cilantro.
Garnish with lime wedges. Serve with black beans, rice, and top with Cholula.

Texas BBQ Shrimp

8 16/20 size shrimp, peeled, deveined, tail on
8 bacon slices, cut in half
8 pickled jalapeno rings*
3 Tbsp Cattleman KC classic BBQ sauce
1-2 lemons, cut into wedges
10 inch bamboo skewers

ASIAN COLESLAW
⅛ cup soy sauce
½ green cabbage, shredded
½ red cabbage, shredded
⅛ cup lime juice
4 carrots, shredded
¼ cup rice vinegar
1½ cups mayonnaise
¼ cup minced mint
2 Tbsp white sugar

HUSHPUPPIES
1 cup flour
1 cup de-germinated corn meal
1 tsp baking soda
1 Tbsp baking powder
¼ cup cream corn
1 Tbsp jalapenos, minced
1½ cups buttermilk
1 large egg, beaten
oil for frying

Place eight pieces of bacon on cutting board. Place shrimp on top of bacon, and place 1 ring of jalapeno on top of the shrimp. Wrap bacon around the shrimp and make sure the bacon only overlaps a little bit, or the bacon won't cook throughout.

Skewer 4 pieces of the wrapped shrimp on bamboo skewer, and the other four pieces of bacon on the second bamboo skewer.

Cook on grill over high temperature until the bacon is crispy on both side, about 7 minutes on each side. When the bacon is crispy, the shrimp is done.

Remove from the skewer and plate with the BBQ sauce, asian coleslaw, and lemon wedges. Serve with the hushpuppies.

Asian Coleslaw

In a large bowl mix shredded green and red cabbage, and shredded carrots and set aside. In separate bowl mix soy sauce, lime juice, rice vinegar, mayonnaise, minced mint and white sugar and whisk until smooth. Completely coat cabbage and carrot mixture with dressing.

Hushpuppies

Mix flour, corn meal, baking soda and baking powder in large mixing bowl.

Add buttermilk, beaten egg, corn, and jalapenos to dry mixture until a moderately thick paste forms. You don't want it too runny, so add the buttermilk slowly until the right consistency is attained. Drop a dollop into 350 degree oil and Deep Fry for 5-7 minutes, until golden brown and the hushpuppies float to the top of the oil.

Serves 8

PICKLED JALAPENO RINGS You can buy or make them from srcatch. To make your own you will need jalapenos, water, vinegar, sugar, kosher salt, garlic, and oregano.

Heat the ingredients (minus the jalapenos), in a saucepan over high heat, *and bring to a boil. Stir in jalapeno peppers and remove from heat, and let cool for 10 minutes.*

Put peppers into jars, covered with vinegar mixture. Refrigerate until needed.

SILVER STAR CAFE

Jeff and Lisa Ward are longtime Park City locals, Jeff in restaurant operations and Lisa in communications and community development. They started the Silver Star Cafe in 2010, creating a community gathering place. It's a "locals' favorite" focusing on great food, ambiance, service and live acoustic music. It's what they call, "The four legs of our table." The Wards are proud to share this very special place with their guests. It feels like home, and you'll be welcomed as friends. The Silver Star Cafe is truly a hidden gem.

Silver Star Café is an intimate, upscale, rustic cafe with award-winning Roots Cuisine; a contemporary, from-scratch, diverse expression of regional foods and flavors from the American Melting Pot. There is a cozy 50-seat dining room, and in warmer months there's additional dining on the wrap-around outdoor patio and plaza. Dinner is served nightly; lunch Monday through Friday, with brunch on Saturday and Sunday. The Café overlooks the Park City Golf Club, at the base of the Silver Star ski chair at Park City Mountain Resort and trailheads for the Spiro and Armstrong trails. Although there is nothing diner-like about the place, the Food Network chose to feature the Café on its "Diner's, Drive-ins and Dives" television show.

Every Thursday, Friday and Saturday, the Silver Star Café presents an intimate, live music dinner show, with all-acoustic folk, jazz, blues, Americana and bluegrass, showcasing local talented singer-songwriters and musicians, as well as national touring artists.

The Café features full service for wine, beer and craft cocktails, plus 360-degree mountain, town, and golf course views. The food and service are fine-dining, yet warmly welcoming. Come as you are, whether straight from the ski hill or hiking trail, or out for a special celebration. This intimate restaurant fills up fast! Reservations are not accepted for lunch or brunch, but are highly recommended for dinner.

All recipes presented by Silver Star Cafe are gluten-free.

Silver Star Café's chef, Dan Sweisford, is a mad scientist in the kitchen. He's spent his career in award-winning– and James Beard-nominated– kitchens including opening four restaurants for the Garces Restaurant Group in Philadelphia and Chicago. Chef Dan has worked with Utah's Waldorf Astoria, Goldener Hirsch Inn, the Chateaux at Silver Lake, Talisker on Main, and the Sundance Tree Room. Proficient in Latin, Asian, French, Spanish and American cuisines, he teases flavors from the many cultural cuisines of America. Though his skills include scientific technique such as molecular gastronomy and sous vide cooking methods, at Silver Star Café, he prefers focusing on the integrity of food in its natural state, bringing out depth of flavor and nuance that is delicious, healthy, and always with an element of the unexpected.

PG142 PG143 PG144 PG145 PG146

Clams and Corn

1 pound Manila clams, scrubbed and purged
3 fingerling potatoes, roasted
3 cippolini onions
¼ cup fava beans
1 cup potato-corn broth
2 charred scallions

¼ cup white wine
3 tsp butter
1 Tbsp garlic minced
2 Tbsp shallot minced
¼ cup charred corn

POTATO-CORN BROTH
  (for 1 gallon of broth)
3 corn cobs
2 onions
3 garlic cloves
1 cup white wine
1 bay leaf
3 russet potatoes, peeled and chopped
2 gallons water

In a large sauté pan, sweat the garlic, cippolini onions and shallot with the clams.
Once slightly colored, add in the white wine and potato corn broth, and cover.
Once the clams are open, add the butter, fingerling potatoes, fava beans, scallions and charred corn.
Bring liquid to a boil to emulsify the butter.
Season to taste with sea salt
Serve with toasted bread.

Potato Corn Broth
In a large pot, sweat the onions and garlic over low heat until they are soft, but no color.
Add the wine and bring to a boil.
Add in the corn cobs, bay leaf and potatoes.
Once at a boil, add the water, and bring back to a boil.
Reduce heat to a simmer and cook for 1 hour.
Strain and chill.

Ingredients are per person.

Crab and Melon Salad with Tarragon Vinaigrette

2 of your favorite type of melons, shaved thin
2 oz tarragon vinaigrette
1 cup baby arugula
1 cup frisse
2 slices dried sliced Prosciutto

¼ watermelon radish, sliced thin (or 3 to 4 of any radish)
¼ lb fresh crab meat

TARRAGON VINAIGRETTE
2 cups tarragon
1 shallot minced
½ cup white balsamic vinegar
2 cups grapeseed oil
1 Tbsp honey
salt to taste

Tarragon Vinaigrette
In a blender, puree tarragon, shallot, white balsamic vinegar and honey.
Once blended, slowly add in the grapeseed oil.
Season with a pinch of salt.

Dried Prosciutto
Preheat oven to 225 degrees.
On a sheet tray, place a piece of parchment paper and coat with non-stick spray.
Lay out the slices of Prosciutto side by side, but not touching and place into oven for 45 minutes or until crispy. They will get crispier as they cool.
Lay cooked, crispy Prosciutto on paper towels and store at room temperature.

Assembly
In one bowl, mix the shaved melon and crab.
Toss with a pinch of salt and a drizzle of olive oil.
In a second bowl, mix together the arugula, frisse, radish and tarragon vinaigrette.
On a plate or bowl, place a layer of the melon mix.
Place the greens on top.
Crumble the Prosciutto crisps over the top.

Heirloom Tomato Salad
with Burratta and Basil-Cocoa Nib Pesto

1 heirloom tomato, cubed
½ ball Buratta cheese
8 candied olives
1 Tbsp basil seeds
2 Tbsp cocoa nib pesto
1 Tbsp balsamic reduction

PESTO
8 oz fresh basil, chopped fine
⅓ cup shallot, minced
¼ cup minced garlic
¾ cup cocoa nibs
1 cup extra virgin olive oil
¼ cup white balsamic vinegar

CANDIED OLIVES
2 cups Kalamata olives
2 cups sugar plus more sugar for coating
4 cups water

BASIL SEEDS
1 basil seed packet
  (can be found in most Asian markets)
1 cup tomato juice
3 cups water

Pesto

Heat a small sauté pan over medium heat. Add ½ of the oil and garlic. Sauté until the garlic just starts to brown.
Pour into a bowl and add cocoa nibs.
While still warm, add all other ingredients and season to taste with salt.

Candied Olives

Preheat oven to 250 degrees.
In a large pot, bring sugar and water to a boil, stirring constantly. Add the olives and simmer for about 30 minutes.
Strain out the olives and save olive syrup for other yummy uses like desserts and cocktails.
Line a sheet pan with parchment paper and spray with non-stick spray. Pour the olives on to the pan and place into the 250 degree oven to dry, about an hour.
Once dry, place the olives into a medium bowl with sugar and toss while still warm to coat. Then put into an air tight container at room temperature.

Basil Seeds

Add basil seeds and water together, stir, and let sit for 5 minutes. Stir in the tomato juice .

Balsamic Reduction

Boil 1 cup balsamic vinegar until reduced by 2/3. Store at room temperature.

Assembly

Place the Burratta cheese in the middle of a plate and arrange the tomatoes around.
Place the olives around in the tomatoes and spoon the basil seeds and pesto over them.
Drizzle with the balsamic reduction.
Season with coarse sea salt and olive oil.

Pork Osso Bucco with
Coconut Creamed Corn and Tomatillo Salsa

Chicken stock (to cover)
2 carrots, chopped
2 ribs celery, chopped
1 large onion, chopped
2 poblano chilies, chopped
3 bay leaves
3 limes, halved
chopped cilantro for garnish
crumbled Queso Fresco for garnish

PORK SHANK RUB
1 pork shank, per person, about 1lb each
1 cup coriander seed
½ cup cumin seed

¼ cup black peppercorn, whole
½ tsp red chili flake
½ tsp cinnamon powder
1½ tsp garlic powder
1½ Tbsp onion powder
1½ Tbsp oregano, dry
¾ cup kosher salt
¼ cup brown sugar

CREAMED CORN
6 fresh corn cobs or 2 qts frozen corn kernels
1½ cup yellow onion, fine chop
2½ tsp garlic, fine chop
1 tsp black pepper, table grind

½ tsp turmeric
3 14 oz cans coconut milk
2 Tbsp grapeseed oil

FRESH TOMATILLO SALSA
3 cup tomatillos, small dice
2 jalapeno, minced
1 shallot, minced
1 tsp garlic, minced
½ cup cilantro, chopped
1 Tbsp honey
1 tsp kosher salt
2 Tbsp lime juice
salt and pepper

Preheat oven to 325 degrees.

Toast coriander, cumin and peppercorns until aromatic, then cool. Once cooled, grind in a spice grinder and combine with red chili flakes, cinnamon powder, onion powder, oregano, kosher salt, and brown sugar. Tie the pork shanks individually with a piece of twine to hold them together during cooking. Rub the pork generously with spice cure. Let marinate overnight.

In a heavy pan add grapeseed or vegetable oil and brown the pork over medium heat. Once browned, transfer pork to a large roasting pan and add chicken stock, carrot, celery, bay leaf, poblano chilies and a few halved limes. Cover tightly and braise in a 325 oven for 4 hours. Allow to cool in braising liquid.

Creamed Corn

In large pan, heat a small amount of grapeseed oil on high heat until near smoking. Add corn kernnels then scrape bare cob with back of a knife to extract milk, and cook until slightly brown. Add onion, garlic, pepper, turmeric and coconut milk and simmer until corn and onions are tender. Slightly puree half in a food processer and mix back in. Season with salt and pepper.

Fresh Tomatillo Salsa

Combine tomatillos, minced jalapeno, shallot, garlic, chopped cilantro, honey, kosher salt and lime juice. Salt and pepper to taste.

Pork Shanks

Pre-heat an oven to 500 degrees.

Discard any fat from the top. Remove pork from cooled liquid, strain the liquid and cook to reduce by half.

Place the shanks in a pan with about a half inch of the reduced braising liquid. Place the pan in the oven for about 10 minutes or until the liquid is thick.

Place pork on creamed corn, ladle reduced jus on top and finish with tomatillo salsa, chopped cilantro and crumbled queso fresco.

Root Beer Cured Lamb Rack

1 whole lamb rack, cured
2 cups fava beans, peeled
2 cups English peas
1 cup cippolini onions, peeled and quartered
4 small stalks celery, diced
2 Tbsp garlic, minced
8 oz pea greens (substitute arugula or your
   favorite green)

¼ cup Pernod or Absinthe
¼ cup white wine
½ cup butter, cubed plus more for basting
2 Tbsp parsley, chopped
2 Tbsp chives, chopped
2 Tbsp chervil, chopped
2 Tbsp tarragon, chopped
Tbsp grapeseed oil

ROOT BEER CURE
½ cup sarsaparilla bark
⅓ cup sassafras root (food grade)
¼ cup licorice root
2 star anise
½ cup brown sugar
1 cup salt

Toast the sarsaparilla, sassafras, licorice and star anise in a dry pan until aromatic and smoking but not burnt.

Add those ingredients to a blender or spice grinder and grind to a fine powder. Mix in sugar and salt.

Completely coat lamb rack with ground spices and let set overnight in refrigerator.

Preheat oven to 450 degrees.

In a large sauté pan, coat the bottom of the pan with grapeseed or vegetable oil. Set over low heat.

Knock any excess cure from the lamb and place fat side down in the pan.

Immediately transfer the pan to the oven, and cook for 10 minutes.

Flip the rack over and cook 5 more minutes. Check the temperature: the internal temperature should be 125 degrees.

While the lamb is cooking, coat another large sauté pan with oil.

Add the onions and garlic, and sweat over medium heat.

Once you see some slight color, add in the fava beans, peas, pea greens and Pernod.

Flame off the Pernod, then add the celery, wine and butter.

Bring to a boil.

When the butter emulsifies and the sauce starts to thicken, toss in the herbs and remove from the heat.

Once the lamb reaches an internal temperature of 125 degrees, remove from the oven and place back on a high burner.

Add a few tablespoons of butter and baste the lamb by spooning the butter over it. Do this for about 2 minutes then set the lamb on a rack to rest at room temperature for at least 5 minutes.

Pour the pan of vegetables and sauce into a shallow bowl, slice the lamb in between the bones and fan out over the vegetables.

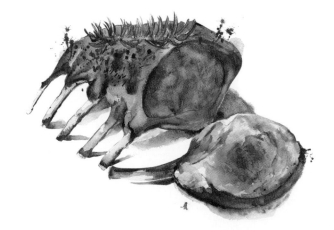

THE BRASS TAG

DV

The Brass Tag restaurant is Deer Valley Resort's first year-round evening operation. It opened in July 2014 and features Deer Valley-inspired brick oven cuisine, including fresh seafood skillets, seared meats, oven roasted fresh fish, locally sourced produce, seasonal flatbreads and specialty sides. The restaurant's name was chosen in keeping with Deer Valley Resort's rich mining history. Miners used brass tags hung on a board to check in and out of work in the mines. If a brass tag remained on the board at the end of a shift, then everyone knew to launch a search.

The Brass Tag is located in The Lodges at Deer Valley; its physical location sits on an old mining claim. The restaurant space itself was designed to give the diner a feeling of being in an old mine shaft; dark wood beams crisscross the ceiling and metal accents are used throughout.

Much of the décor also features actual mine history: the bar is inlaid with a map of Deer Valley and Park City mine claims and historical photos adorn the walls. The heart of the restaurant is the brick oven; where diners can delight in watching their favorite dishes finish in the oven.

The Brass Tag is a great spot for an après ski craft cocktail and creative snack. House favorites include the Oven Fried Chimichurri chips and gooey skillet cookies. It's comfort food, but with a Deer Valley twist. The Brass Tag is home to the winner of the Park City Area Restaurant Association's 2015 Summer Cocktail Contest. Be sure to try the Evangeline, a gin cocktail created by restaurant manager and bartender Josh Hockman.

JODIE ROGERS

Jodie Rogers, the executive chef of Snow Park and Empire Canyon Lodges, is a native of Australia. After five seasons at Deer Valley serving as the manager of the employee dining program and as sous chef at Snow Park Lodge, she was promoted to Snow Park Executive Chef in December 2000, the Empire Canyon Lodge in 2002, the Deer Valley Grocery~Café in 2010 and most recently, executive chef at The Brass Tag at the Lodges at Deer Valley in 2014.

Rogers' 20-year cooking career includes stints in several hotels in Sydney, Australia and as head chef at Australia's Charlotte Pass Resort. In 1994 and 1998 she was part of the cooking teams that took the Australian Salon Culinaire Restaurant of Champions gold medal. She successfully opened Toast Bar and Restaurant in London, England in 1999. Rogers' was invited to cook on NBC's *Today Show* in March of 2014.

Rogers favorite activities include skiing, snowshoeing, mountain biking, running half marathons, hiking, traveling, rock climbing, and cooking with her kids.

PG152 PG153 PG154

Oven Fired Chimichurri Chips

potato chips, homemade or any store bought
  potato chip or pita chip will work
2 oz chimichurri sauce
¼ cup crispy bacon chopped
1 oz of each of th following cheeses, grated
  Deer Valley uses:
  Beehive seahive cheddar
  Beehive Seahive semi soft cheddar (substitute Jarlsburg if needed)
  Gruyere

CHIMICHURRI SAUCE
½ cup parsley
2 Tbsp red wine vinegar
½ tsp garlic, pureed
⅓ tsp red pepper flakes
2 ½ Tbsp fresh oregano
½ lemon, zested and juiced
2 tsp sherry vinegar
3 ½ Tbsp extra virgin olive oil
salt and pepper

Chimichurri Sauce

Add parsley, red wine vinegar, garlic, red pepper flakes, oregano, lemon and sherry vinegar to a food processor and pulse to combine.
Once the mixture is smooth, slowly add in olive oil.
Add salt and pepper to taste.

Assembly

Assemble the chips, the cheeses, and crispy bacon on an oven safe dish. Bake until cheese is nicely melted. Top off with Chimichurri sauce and green onions.

Chef's Notes

The Oven Fired Chimichurri Chips served at The Brass Tag is the chef's take on a classic nacho dish. Using housemade potato chips, Niman Ranch bacon, garden fresh herbs and local cheeses, this dish supports local businesses and satisfies all that are able to enjoy. This comfort food has inspired the Deer Valley Resort Bakery to use a chimichurri variation in a Mariposa dessert.

Start to finish: 15 minutes
Serves 1

Brick Oven Shrimp Skillet with Saffron Roasted Red Pepper Sauce

1 lb raw shrimp, 24-30 count/lb
  peeled and deveined

SAFFRON ROASTED RED PEPPER SAUCE
1 roasted red bell pepper, peeled,
  seeded and cored, roughly chopped

1 Tbsp shallots, minced
1 tsp saffron threads
¼ cup white wine
12 Tbsp butter, at room temperature
1 tsp olive oil
1 tsp grapeseed oil (or other preferred

high smoke point oil)
1 crusty baguette
1 Tbsp fresh herbs of your choice,
  for garnish
salt and pepper to taste

In a large saucepan, sweat the shallots in the olive oil until translucent. Add wine and reduce by half. Once reduced, add the saffron and red bell pepper and cook until almost all of the liquid is evaporated. Remove mixture from heat and transfer to a blender or food processor. Add the butter and blend or process until completely smooth. Put the mixture in the refrigerator (this mixture will keep up to one week refrigerated or a couple months frozen).

Add the grapeseed oil to a warm sauté pan. Add shrimp and season with salt and pepper. Cook until barely pink, about one minute. Add all of the butter mixture to the pan and stir rapidly to create a smooth sauce and finish cooking the shrimp. When the shrimp make a "C" shape, they are completely cooked (but don't let them become an "O" as that means they're overcooked).

To finish, top with herbs. Serve with crusty bread.

Serves 5 - 6

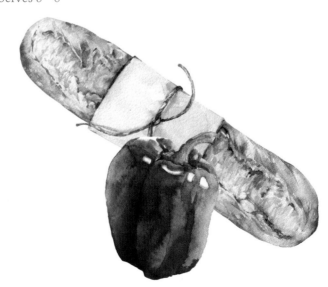

Cheddar Truffle Chive Spätzle

SPÄTZLE
1 tsp salt
1 pinch nutmeg
1 Tbls chives
½ cup semolina flour
½ cup water
1 cup all purpose flour
2 eggs lightly, scrambled

CHEESE SAUCE
6 cups heavy cream
3 cups very sharp white cheddar, shredded
¼ cup blond roux
  (equal parts flour to butter)

TO FINISH THE SPÄTZLE
¼ cup bread cumbs
1 tbsp chives
1 cup cheese blend
  (Gruyere and cheddar)
drizzle of truffle oil (optional)

Spätzle

With a fork, blend the wet and dry ingredients in the following order: salt, nutmeg, chives, semolina flour, water, all-purpose flour and eggs. Rest dough for 15 minutes. The consistency should be thicker than pancake batter but wetter than biscuit dough.

Moisten a heat-proof board with a smooth surface, like a wooden cutting board, with cool water.

Spread some of the batter on the board in a long strip, going from one end of the board to the other.

Cut off small, thin strips of the batter and drop them into boiling water. Cut the dough at small angles to keep the spätzle from getting too long (they will almost double in size as they cook). As you cut the dough, let the small bits drop into the boiling water. If the dough doesn't want to release from your spatula, just wet the spatula with cool water.

You can also cook the spätzle directly in broth.

Once the spätzle floats, let them cook at a gentle boil for another minute or two. The spätzle should have a pleasantly firm texture, not tough and chewy, and no raw flour taste. Cooking time will differ depending on the size of your spätzle. Shock the cooked spätzle in ice water briefly. Remove and set aside.

Cheese Sauce

In a saucepan, bring the cream to a simmer. Slowly whisk in cheddar cheese until fully incorporated. If you own a Vita Mix or high power blender you can do this process in the blender. After the cheese is fully incorporated, whisk in the roux. Let the sauce cool completely.

Reserve one cup of white sauce and mix the remainder with the cold spätzle. Put spätzle mixture in a casserole dish. Spread reserved sauce over spätzle. Sprinkle with cheese blend and bread crumbs. Bake at 375°F for 15 to 20 minutes. When the edges of the dish bubble, remove from oven and sprinkle with chives and truffle oil to finish.

THE BRIDGE CAFE & GRILL

OWNER EMERSON CRUZ DE OLIVEIRA

For seven years the Bridge Cafe & Grill has been serving American food with a Brazilian flair. Located directly at the bottom of the Town Lift on Main Street, it has one of Park City's best patios for spectacular outdoor dining. You can ski-in / ski-out to the front door in the winter, or hop on the Town Lift for a scenic after-dinner chairlift ride in the summer.

Freeskier Magazine wrote, "We voted The Bridge as one of the Best Breakfast Restaurants in Park City on Taste of Park City for 2011." They serve more omelets than burgers, and serve breakfast all day. Try out the Brazuca omelet, with fillings ranging from mushrooms to bacon to pecans and strawberries. Or make a morning feast out of the Cristo Redentor; a French-toast style ham and swiss cheese sandwich.

For a tasty lunch appetizer, order the unique Coxinhas; balls of chicken salad shaped into drumsticks. Or snack on the Camarao a Brazuca; sauteed garlic shrimp with fresh tomatoes, herbs and onions. Wash that all down with a pint of one of twenty local and imported beers.

For dinner, have a chipotle burger, or the Moqueca Baiana; a combination of fish, shrimp, mussels, clams, tomatoes, and onions in coconut milk, served over rice. You won't get that anywhere else in town. Sip on Brazilian sodas, or try a traditional Mojito or a pineapple mint Caipirinha on the deck before hand.

The Bridge is well known for hosting big events and wedding ceremonies on their deck, from private parties up to 500 guests to the Tour De Suds bike race. During the holidays, watch Santa Claus descend the Town Lift with his reindeer to the waiting crowd!

The Bridge Cafe & Grill is a gathering place like no other in Park City.

Emerson Oliveira is originally from Brazil, and came to Park City 5 years ago for a work experience project.

After graduating with a computer science degree in his native country, he made the move to Park City.

He decided to stay in Park City, and headed back to school to learn English.

Emerson worked in many Park City restaurants, before starting The Bridge Cafe & Grill with two partners in 2008.

Today, he is the sole owner, and with the help of his wife, Juliana Klein, and his landlords, the Sweeney Brothers, he made The Bridge Café a success.

He says, "In 2011 I bought the Flying Sumo Sushi and now, I am hungry for more."

Coxinhas

MS | **A**

1½ pounds chicken breasts, boneless, skinless
4-5 cups of chicken broth
1 carrot
2 onions
2 bay leaves

2 Tbsp butter
2 cloves garlic
1 lime, juiced
1 8-ounce package of cream cheese, softened
2-3 cups of flour

2 eggs
2-3 cups of very finely
   grated bread crumbs
vegetable oil for frying
salt and pepper to taste

Place chicken breasts in a large shallow pot. Cover with chicken broth, adding water if necessary keeping chicken breasts covered by at least ½ inch of liquid.

Add the carrot, one of the onions (peeled and halved) as well as the bay leaves.

Bring liquid to a gentle simmer, and cook for 15 to 20 minutes, or until chicken is just cooked through (barely pink in the middle of the thickest part).

Set chicken aside to cool, and strain and reserve the broth. Shred the chicken into very small pieces. A food processor fitted with the plastic blade works great, but you can also use your fingers.

Stir the softened cream cheese and lime juice into the shredded chicken.

Finely chop the second onion and the garlic. Sauté the onion and garlic in 2 tablespoons of butter until golden and soft.

Add the hot onions and garlic to the chicken mixture and stir until everything is well mixed.

Measure the chicken broth. If you have less than three cups, add more canned chicken broth to make 3 cups. In a sauce pan bring the chicken broth to a boil, and gradually stir in an equal amount of flour as you have broth.

Stir vigorously and cook for 2 to 3 minutes. Mixture will become a stiff dough. Remove from heat, chill in refrigerator for 1 hour.

At this point, you can chill the chicken mixture and the dough for several hours or overnight.

To shape the coxinhas: take a piece of the dough about the size of a golf ball with floured hands. Roll it into a ball, then hollow out the middle for the filling.

Press a golf ball size (about 1½ tablespoons) piece of the chicken filling inside the ball of dough, and press the dough closed around the filling. Shape into an approximate drumstick shape, 3 to 4 inches tall, flouring hands as necessary.

Stand the coxinhas on a baking sheet, so that the pointed end sticks upwards. Continue until you run out of dough or filling. Whisk the eggs together in a bowl. Place the bread crumbs in a shallow pan (like a cake pan) and season with salt and pepper. Dip the coxinhas in the egg, then in the breadcrumbs to coat. Chill the breaded coxinhas for 1 hour.

Fill a heavy-bottomed pot with enough oil to cover the coxinhas. Heat the oil to 360 degrees. Fry the coxinhas in batches until deep golden brown.

Serve warm.

Makes 24 coxinhas.

COXINHAS are a popular street food snack in Brazil. Savory dough shaped into a drumstick around a creamy chicken salad filling, then battered and fried. "I didn't quite know what to make of them the first time I tried them," says owner Cruz de Oliviera, "but they really are an ingenious street food. They're easy to eat on the go, they're a meal unto themselves. They have a unique appearance (simulated drumstick), and most importantly, they are deep fried and delicious."

Brazilian Passion Salad

SALAD
1 bag of mixed greens, spinach or arugula
handful of grape tomatoes
¼ slice of red onions, sliced in rings
½ Yukon gold potato, julienne

DRESSING
2 oz passion fruit puree
2 oz extra virgin olive oil
2 oz water
2 Tbsp of sugar
salt & black pepper

Gently wash all of the salad greens, then dry in a salad spinner until completely dry.
If not using the greens right away, store them wrapped loosely in paper towels and set aside.

Potato Sticks
Julienne cut the Yukon gold potatoes, put into a bowl with cold water. After the potatoes are in cold water for about 3 minutes, drain the water and let it rest on a paper towel.
Heat a pan with canola oil and deep fry the potatoes until golden brown and let them rest on a paper for crispness.
In a bowl toss the mixed greens, grape tomatoes and red onions with 2 tablespoons of passion fruit dressing.
Serve on a plate and garnish with the potato sticks.

Dressing
Slowly blend the passion fruit puree, with olive oil, salt, pepper, 2 ounces of water and 2 tablespoons of sugar.
Add more sugar to taste if necessary.

MARACUJÁ In Brazil, the term maracujá applies to passion fruit (maracujá azedo, or "sour") and granadillo (maracujá doce, or "sweet"). Passion fruit mousse is a common dessert, and passion fruit pulp is routinely used to decorate the tops of cakes. Passion fruit juice, ice pops and more *recently soft drinks are also popular. On this salad recipe, passion fruit is a key ingredient for our dressing.*

Moqueca Baiana

4 cutlets blue eye cod, or firm fish
  with similar texture
8 oz prawns, head removed
6 oz calamari, cut in rings (or clams)
2 cups fish stock
¾ cup coconut milk

1 red bell pepper, sliced in rings
1 yellow pepper, sliced in rings
3 tomatoes, sliced in rings
2 small onions, sliced in rings
1 small onion, roughly chopped
3 cloves garlic, crushed

1 lime, juiced
1 red chili, chopped
2 Tbsp palm oil
chopped parsley for garnishing
black pepper
salt

Place the fish cutlets into a large bowl. Season them with the lime juice, salt, black pepper, and garlic. Set aside to marinate for 20 minutes.

In a separate bowl, season prawns and calamari with salt and pepper.

Heat the palm oil in the clay-pot and fry the chopped onion until golden brown. Remove the pot from heat.

Layer the rest of the onions, bell peppers and tomatoes on top of the fish cutlets.

Sprinkle it with the rest of parsley and red chiles.
Pour coconut milk and fish stock into the clay-pot.
Bring mixture to a boil, simmer gently while covered, for 15 minutes.
Remove the lid. Add the calamari rings and prawns.
Stir gently and simmer for another 15 minutes or until vegetables are tender.

MOQUECA BAIANA *is a seafood stew original from the native people of Brazil, slowly cooked in a clay-pot and made with some of the freshest ingredients.*

The dish evolved during the Colonial Brazil times when the Portuguese brought coconuts to the country (and planted the coconut trees along the coast in replacement for the prime wood that was taken), while the African slaves introduced palm oil to the country.

The two variations of dish are the Moqueca Baiana (from

the northeast State of Bahia) and the Moqueca Capixaba (from the Southeast State of Espirito Santo). Coconut milk and palm oil are only used in the Baiana recipe.

Although it is a stew, this dish can be enjoyed year-round so whenever you happen to be in Brazil, or at The Bridge Cafe & Grill in Park City, Utah, enjoy a good Moqueca.

THE FARM
AT CANYONS VILLAGE

THE FARM

CV

Charles "Zeke" Wray

Located in the heart of Canyons Resort Village and overlooking the Ski Beach, The Farm features an innovative menu that focuses on ingredients sourced from local and regional farms and artisan purveyors.

This rustic yet refined restaurant offers both indoor and outdoor dining, and features a welcoming lounge with an amazing selection of wines, including over 250 bottles that recived the 2013 Award of Excellence from Wine Spectator.

When first opened in 2011, The Farm was named the "Best New Restaurant in Utah" by the highly competitive, annual Salt Lake Magazine Dining Awards, and earned a spot as one of the top 25 restaurants in the state of Utah by Salt Lake Magazine in 2015. At The Farm, you'll find fresh menu selections prepared from scratch and using sustainably-raised fare that coincides with the seasons.

The Farm has an extensive small plates menu, with treats such as the Bison Chili, Pickeled Beets and Kale, and Maple Glazed Pork Belly. The large plate menu includes offerings such as the Idaho Sturgeon with Cider and Bacon Braised Cabbage and Smoked Cauliflower Puree. Try the Broccoli Casserole, Tomahawk Pork Chop, or Pan-Braised Chicken and Dumplings.

Park City Mountain Resort and Canyons Resort combined in the summer of 2015-2016 to create the largest single ski and snowboard resort in the United States. The new, 8 passenger Quicksilver Gondola connection, along with the new Miners Camp Restaurant, King Con Express six-pack and Motherlode Express quad made up just some of the resort improvements totaling over $50 million for the 2015-16 season. With over 7,300 acres, 300+ trails, 41 lifts, six terrain parks, one super pipe and one mini pipe, plus many diverse ski-in/ski-out and village adjacent lodging properties, Park City is an easily accessible, world-class mountain destination located in an authentic and historic western town.

Park City Executive Chef Zeke Wray stumbled into the kitchen at age 15 and quickly discovered his passion for the world of food.

Zeke studied at the California Culinary Academy in San Francisco, learning the principles that have allowed him to develop and refine his passion and interests.

The mountains lured Wray to Park City where he assisted in opening a dozen different eateries. After a move to Arizona in 2009, Zeke was recruited by Canyons Resort, where he was appointed Canyons' executive chef in 2012, and two years later as the Senior Director of Hospitality Food and Beverage.

Zeke continues to serve in this role at Park City Mountain after Canyons and Park City Mountain Resort combined in 2015 to become the largest ski resort in the United States.

PG160 PG161 PG162 PG163 PG164

Farm Cheese with Pickled Strawberries and Walnuts

	PICKLED STRAWBERRIES	PICKLING LIQUID	PICKLED WALNUTS
16 cups whole milk	1 pint basket strawberries	3 cups hot water	1 cup walnuts, chopped
1 cup heavy cream	4 cups pickling liquid	1 cups champagne vinegar	1 cup pickling liquid
1½ Tbsp citric acid	handful fresh basil	1 cup sugar	1 Tbsp pickling spice
1½ Tbsp salt		3 Tbsp salt	water
¼ cup water			

Farm Cheese

Dissolve citric acid in water. Combine milk, cream, salt and stir in the citric acid.

Slowly heat up to 170 degrees or until you get a firm curd. You don't want the liquid to get too hot, or the cheese will be dry and grainy.

When curd forms, take off the heat and cut cheese with a long knife into 2 inch stripes. Let rest for 20 minutes.

Remove curds with a skimmer into a strainer layered with cheese cloth and dripping bowl.

Refrigerate overnight. Remove cheese out of cheese cloth and fill into desired container. Cheese will be good for up to one week.

Pickling Liquid

Bring water, champagne vinegar, sugar and salt to a quick boil. Let cool.

Pickling Spice

Mix spice with water and on medium heat, simmer, then strain.

Pickled Strawberries

Wash strawberries very well and remove the top part and cut into halves. Transfer into a bowl with the basil and pour the pickling liquid over the strawberries. Cover and let cool.

Pickled Walnuts

Use the same method as the pickled strawberries. Place chopped walnuts into a bowl and cover with hot pickling liquid. Cover the bowl and let cool.

Serve the Farm Cheese with grilled bread, local honey, pickled walnuts and strawberries.

A Farm staple, this easy to make cheese has endless possibilities to substitute for any soft cheese in recipes.

PICKLING SPICE This spice can either be bought in the store or you can make your own by mixing: 2 tablespoons mustard seed, 1 tablespoon whole allspice, 2 teaspoons coriander seeds, 2 whole cloves, 1 teaspoon ground ginger, 1 teaspoon crushed red pepper flakes, 1 bay leaf, crumbled, 1 cinnamon stick (2 inches).

French Onion Soup

10 sweet onions, julienne cut
¼ cup grapeseed oil
½ cup balsamic vinegar
1 cup sherry wine
6 quarts veal stock
1 pinch chili flakes

fresh thyme
bay leaf
salt and pepper to taste
fresh minced chives for garnish

SMOKED CHEDDAR CROSTONE
4 slices toasted baguette
4 slices of Gold Creek smoked cheddar

Caramelize onions in the grapeseed oil on low heat for 3-5 hours. The slower the better, until the onions are a dark golden color but not burnt.

Deglaze with balsamic vinegar and mix well. Raise the heat and reduce the balsamic by half. The addition of balsamic vinegar and sherry wine gives this classic soup a unique bite. Add sherry wine and reduce by half.

Tie the thyme and by leaf together with butcher twine.
Add the thyme-bay leaf wrap and the stock.
Bring to a boil and reduce to a simmer.
Simmer 45 minutes to 1 hour.
Finish with salt and pepper, and season with red chili flakes.

Smoked Cheddar Crostone
Place the slices of cheese on the toasted baguette and melt under broiler.

Assembly
For each serving pour a 6 ounce portion of soup into a soup bowl, and place one crostone on top.
Finish with fresh cut chives.

Note: If want to add any braised meatslike oxtail or short rib you can substitute the veal stock with the braising liquid.

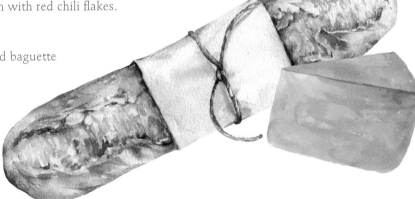

CROSTONE *Crostone are a larger version of crostini or bruschetta. Slices of bread are toasted or grilled, then covered with any of various savory toppings of cheeses, meats, or vegetables, or used to garnish soup or salad.*

Roasted Beets and Honey

4 beets
2 Tbsp extra virgin olive oil
salt, pepper to taste
¼ cup cream cheese, softened
2 cups whole milk ricotta
2 Tbsp heavy cream
6 Tbsp honey
salt, pepper to taste

1 cup walnuts, toasted
½ cup lemon vinaigrette
arugula
salt, pepper to taste

LEMON VINAIGRETTE
½ cup extra virgin olive oil
1 tsp lemon zest, grated (microplane)
⅓ cup lemon Juice
2 gloves garlic, minced
1 tsp sugar
½ tsp salt
½ tsp pepper

Toss beets in extra virgin olive oil until just lightly coated. Season with salt and pepper and wrap in aluminum foil and roast in oven at 400 degrees until soft.
Remove beets from oven and rub with paper towel to peel.
Let cool to room temperature.
When cool, cut beets to desired shape.

In the bowl of a mixer fitted with a whisk attachment, beat cream cheese until smooth and pliable.
Add ricotta, cream and honey. Beat on medium speed for 4 to 5 minutes until mixture is less grainy and fluffy.
Season with a little bit of salt and pepper.

LEMON VINAIGRETTE
In a small mason jar combine olive oil, lemon zest, lemon juice, minced garlic, sugar, and salt and pepper. Screw on lid and shake very well.

Assembly
To serve, spread the ricotta with a rubber spatula evenly on each plate.
Layer the beets randomly on top of the ricotta.
Dress the Arugula with the lemon vinaigrette and season with salt and pepper.
Space the arugula between the beets and finish the salad with a drizzle of aged balsamic vinegar and the toasted walnuts.

Try substituting farm cheese, see recipe on page 168, for the ricotta. If you don't like beets you can substitute any root vegetable for the beets.

Butternut Squash Ravioli

PASTA DOUGH
2 cups all purpose Flour
2 cups 00 Flour (an italian finer ground flour)
3 eggs
1 Tbsp salt
olive oil

BUTTERNUT FILLING
1 butternut squash, peeled and diced
3 Tbsp heavy cream
1 onion cut, bruinoise (short Julienne)
2 Tbsp butter
3 Tbsp parmesan, grated
1 pinch nutmeg

RAVIOLI
8 Tbsp butter
20 fresh sage leaves
2 egg yolks, beaten
1 cup pancetta, cut into strips
  and crisped like bacon

Pasta Dough

Make a hole in the center of the flours and add the eggs. Using a fork, beat the eggs together and then begin to incorporate the flour, starting from inside to outside.

When half of the flour is incorporated, the dough will begin to come together. Start kneading the dough with the palms of your hands. Once the dough has come together, set the dough aside and discard any dried bits of dough. Continue kneading for 10 minutes, dusting the board with additional flour as necessary. The dough should be elastic and a little sticky.

Wrap the dough in plastic wrap and allow to rest 24 hours in refrigerator.

Butternut Filling

Peel and dice butternut squash.

Toss in Extra Virgin Olive oil and season with salt and pepper. Roast in oven at 350F until soft.

Place in blender and puree with heavy cream, until smooth. Melt butter in pan and cook onions until soft.

Add butternut squash puree and cook for about 3 minutes until slightly dry.

Remove from heat and stir in the parmesan cheese and nutmeg. Cool completely.

Ravioli

Bring a big pot with salted water to a boil. Roll out the dough with a pasta machine. Start with your machine at thickness 9 and work your way down to thickness 2.

Cut the dough into 3 inch squares; each ravioli needs 2 squares. For each of the ravioli brush one square with egg yolk and place about 2 teaspoons of filling in the middle.

Cover with another pasta square and tightly seal the edges around the filling making sure the ravioli is completely closed.

Cook the ravioli in the boiling salted water for about 2-3 minutes until pasta is 'al dente'. Remove ravioli from water and drain well.

In a large sautée pan melt butter and let slightly brown. Add the sage leaves and fry them in the melted butter until crispy, make sure not to burn the sage. Remove sage and set aside. Gently combine the drained ravioli with the brown butter and the crisped pancetta.

Season with salt, pepper and garnish with the crispy sage.

Finish with fresh grated parmesan cheese.

Herbed Spaetzle

SPAETZLE
3 cups flour
2 cups milk
1 cup eggs
1 Tbsp salt
¼ cup parsley, chopped
¼ cup chives, chopped
¼ cup chervil, chopped

SAUCE
1 cup black trumpet mushrooms, cleaned
1 cup Emmenthaler cheese, grated
½ cup white wine
½ cup caramelized onions
1 Tbsp shallots, minced
1 Tbsp garlic, minced
1 cup heavy cream
1 Tbsp butter
¼ cup parsley, chopped

¼ cup chives, chopped
¼ cup chervil, chopped
nutmeg to taste
salt, pepper to taste

CRISPY FRIED SHALLOTS
3 whole shallots
1 cup buttermilk
1 cup flour
¼ cup grapeseed oil

Spaetzle
Combine flour, milk, eggs, salt, chopped parsley, chopped chives and chopped chervil in mixer. Mix with paddle on high for 2 minutes.
In a large pot bring salted water to a boil.
To make spaetzle forms, press dough through spaetzle maker, or a large holed sieve or metal grater into boiling water.
Cook spaetzle for 3 minutes and shock in ice water.
Drain and dry

Sauce
Melt butter in sautée pan and sear spaetzle and mushrooms until light brown.
Add garlic and shallots and deglaze with white wine.
Reduce wine all the way.
Add heavy cream and bring to a boil.
Add Emmenthaler cheese and toss quickly until creamy.
Season with salt, pepper and nutmeg to taste.
Finish with parsley, chives, and chervil.
Garnish with crispy fried shallots

Crispy Fried Shallots
Heat ¼ inch of oil over medium-high heat in a small saucepan. Clean shallots and slice into rings. Soak the shallot rings in butter milk and dredge in flour.

Place shallot rings into the oil to cook until light golden brown, about 8 minutes, remove when they are browned and crispy. Remove the shallots using a slotted spoon. To drain, place the shallots on a plate layered with paper towel.

WINE DIVE

P

CHEF PARKER

Don't be fooled by the name: this is anything but a dive. It's an upscale, innovatively decorated annex adjacent to Boneyard Saloon and Kitchen, with cool colors, large windows, and comfy seating. The Wine Dive is an urban lounge plunked down in the middle of the mountains, with intimate tables, lounge areas, and counter seating. It's a place to meet up with friends, enjoy a few beverages, and partake of a number of tasty small dishes and drinks.

Watch Chef Parker prepare pizzas, charcuterie boards, small bit plates, and imaginative combinations in his new exhibition kitchen and wood-fired oven. This rocking oven produces wonderful, magical treats right before your eyes; it's theatre, art and fine dining combined with a completely sexy menu. Try the Rock Shrimp Pesto Pizza to start, or the Guac' n Lobster Tacos, or ask your server to recommend a charcuterie board or daily special. With a expansive small plate menu designed for sampling and sharing. Wine Dive is a social dining experience that will delight friends and foodies alike.

If you're thirsty, there are more fine beers, cocktails, and wines than you can safely drink at one sitting. Choose from the largest selection of craft beers in town, or try one of the 16 varietal wines on tap, using the latest technology to keep keg wines absolutely fresh, or try one of the 80 bottled wines from both the old and new world.

On warm days, the windows rise up to open beds of fresh flowers and mountain air. There is plenty of free parking, and you're just a few minutes from the hustle and bustle of Park City's Main Street.

Chris Parker has a fine touch with food and the art of food. It's evident as you watch him meticulously prepare items for both Boneyard Saloon & Kitchen, and Wine Dive.

Starting at the age of 15 as a dishwasher, he was soon cooking.

Before coming to Park City, Chris has cooked in New Orleans, in Santa Barbara, California and in Maui where he was Executive Sous Chef under renowned Chef Mark Ellman. Chris also spent two years working under Chef Brent Holleman, who apprenticed under Paul Bocuse, who is considered an ambassodor of modern French Cuisine.

He says, "My style of cooking comes from the experience through my career. Food is my life and wouldn't have it any other way."

PG178 PG179 PG180

Guac n' Lobster Tacos

1 lb slipper lobster tails, removed from shells
¼ cup Maine lobster claws and knuckle meat
1 cup white wine
1 lemon, juiced
1 bay leaf
parsley stems
pinch of peppercorns
ice water
wonton Wraps

GUACAMOLE
1 avocado
¼ cup cilantro
1 cup tomato, chopped
1 jalapeno, chopped
2 Tbsp red onion, chopped
1 lime, juiced
salt and pepper to taste

CILANTRO AIOLI
1 bunch cilantro
½ cup mayonnaise
1 lime, Juiced
½ jalapeno, seeded and diced
2 Tbsp honey
salt and Pepper to taste

Poach lobster meat in 2 cups of water, white wine, lemon juice, bay leaf, parsley and peppercorns. Poach for 5 minutes. Shock in ice bath. Cut into small pieces and mix with guacamole.

Guacamole
Mix together avocado, chopped cilantro, jalapeno, red onion, ½ cup of the diced tomoato, lime juice and salt and pepper to taste.

Fry wonton wraps into taco shells.

Aioli Puree
Puree in blender or food processor, cilantro, mayonnaise, lime juice, honey, jalapeno and salt and pepper to taste.

Stuff shells with lobster and guacamole mix, serve with aioli on side and other ½ cup of diced tomatocs. Enjoy!

Rock Shrimp, Prosciutto, Mojo Verde Green Tomato and White Cheddar Pizza

3½ oz rock shrimp, per serving
   peeled an deveined
¼ cup prosciutto, chopped sliced
½ cup white cheddar cheese

PIZZA DOUGH
4 cups warm water
½ Tbsp yeast
1 Tbsp salt
3½ lbs Caputo pizza flour (00 flour)

PIZZA SAUCE
2 green tomatoes
½ cup cilantro leaves
3 garlic cloves, chopped
1 jalapeno, chopped
½ cup lime juice
¼ cup olive oil
1 Tbsp cumin
salt and pepper to taste

Preheat oven to 600 degrees.
Clean Rock Shrimp, slice prosciutto, and grate white cheddar cheese.

Pizza Dough
Mix 80 percent of the Caputo pizza flour with the water, yeast, salt.Knead in the remaining 20 percent of the flour and mix for 4 minutes. Cover and let rest for 2 hours then ball out 6.5 oz.

Pizza Sauce
Combine the yeast with the water.
Blend Green tomatoes, cilantro, garlic, jalapeno, lime juice, olive oil, cumin and salt and pepper to taste.
Toss dough in to pizza round and place raw rock shrimp, prosciutto pieces, sauce and white cheddar on top.
Bake in pizza oven at 600 degrees until crispy. Enjoy!.

Assembly
Toss a ball of dough into a flat pizza round. Top with the sauce, the shrimp and prosciutto and then the cheese. Bake in pizza oven until done and crispy.

Cherry Sage, and Corn Bread Stuffed Quail

1 quail
¼ cup dried cherries
¼ cup bacon bits
1 Tbsp sage chopped
1 Tbsp pine nuts
¼ cup chicken stock
demi-glace (store bought)
¼ cup cornbread muffin crumbles
¼ chablis wine

CORN BREAD MUFFINS
1 ¼ cup flour
⅔ cup cormeal
⅓ cup sugar
1 Tbsp baking powder
½ tsp salt
2 cups milk
½ cup canola oil

QUINOA
1 cup quinoa
2 cup water
salt and pepper to taste

Corn Bread Muffins
Pre heat oven to 400 degrees.
Mix together flour, cornmeal. sugar, baking powder, and salt.
Add milk and canola oil and mix well. Bake at 400 degrees
for 30 min.

Stuffing
Rehydrate dried cherries in chablis wine. Save cherry liquid.
Stuff each quail with stuffing.
Mix together cornbread muffin crumbles, dried cherries,
bacon, chopped sage, pine nuts and chicken stock.

Roast in oven at 450 degrees for about 8 minutes.
Combine cherry liquid and demi-glace. Heat and simmer to
reduce by ⅓. Demi glace is available at grocery stores.

Quinoa
Boil 2 cups of water add quinoa simmer for 15 min. then cover
turn off heat and rest for 4 min.
Serve over a bed of quinoa and drizzle
demi-glace on top. Enjoy!

Restaurant Address and Contact Information

 Canyons Village   Deer Valley   Kamas   Main Street   Off Main Street   Prospector   Silver Lake   Silver Star

Book and Jacket design and Production by: Lauren Nadler
Editor: Pam Archbold; Photographer: Pat Cone

Photography and Illustration Credits: Cover, White Barn, Lauren Nadler; Park City Town Map, Roger Burrows; pg 1, 350 Main, Pat Cone; pg 2 Black Sesame Sea Scallops, Pat Cone; pg 8, Backside of Wasatch Crest, Lauren Nadler; pg 9, Boneyard, Pat Cone; pg 10, Pork Belly Lettuce Wraps, Pat Cone; pg 15, Lte Fall Park City, Pat Cone; pg 16, Winter Scene, Pat Cone; pg 17, Butchers, Pat Cone; pg 18, Filet Oscar, Pat Cone, pg 23, Olympic Park, Pat Cone; pg 24 White Barn at Silver Springs, Phil Archbold; pg 32, Jupiter Peak, Lauren Nadler; pg 41, Fly Fishing Weber River, Lauren Nadler; ; 42 Jupiter Peak, Lauren Nadler; pg 43, Flanagan's On Main, Pat Cone; pg 51, Flanagan's on Main, Lauren Nadler; pg 52, Thaynes Canyon Mine Building, Lauren Nadler; pg 59, Top of Jupiter Peak looking down Machetes, Lauren Nadler; pg 60, Hot Air Balloons, Lauren Nadler; pg 61-63 Gateway Grille Photos, Daren Wharton; pg 67, Tour od Utah, Lauren Nadler; pg 68, Wind Swept Jupiter Peak, Lauren Nadler; pg 70, Goldener Hirsch Fondue, Pat Cone; pg 71, Fondue, Tamahawk Pork Chop, Apple Strudel, Pat Cone; pg 75, End of Day View for Patrol, Lauren Nadler; pg 76, Aspen Trees, Park City Mountain Resort, Lauren Nadler; pg 77, Good Karma, Pat Cone; pg 84, Miners Hospital, Lauren Nadler; pg 85-87, All Photos No Name Saloon and Grill, Pat Cone; pg 91, McPolin Barn, Lauren Nadler; pg 92, Tour de Suds, Lauren Nadler; pg 93 and 95, Lobster and Gnocci, Becky Rosenthal; pg 102 Mid Mountain Miners Buildings, Pat Cone; pg 108, Fall Dusting on Ski Team Ridge, Pat Cone; pg 117 Park City Mountain Resort and Ski Team Ridge Fall Colors, Lauren Nadler; pg 118, Park Ave Color, Lauren Nadler; pg 128, Desolation Lake, Lauren Nadler; pg 129, Sammy's Bistro, Pat Cone; pg 131, Texas BBS Shrimp, Pat Cone; pg 137, White Barn, Phil Archbold; pg 138 Winter view, Phil Archbold; pg 148 Berrys' on Summer Hike, Phil Archbold; pg 155 Jordanelle Resevoir from Deer Valley, Lauren Nadler; pg 156, Aspens Backside of Guardsmans Pass, Lauren Nadler; pg 157, Town Lift Plaza for Tour de Suds, Lauren Nadler; pg 158-159, Coxhinas, Shutterstock; pg 163, Town Lift Deck Bicycles, Emerson Cruz de Oliveira; pg 164, Home Run in the Morning, Park City Mountain Resort, Lauren Nadler; pg 173, Peak Patrol Shack Summer View, Phil Archbold; pg 174, Dusting on Park City, Phil Archbold; pg 175-177, Wine Dive and all Dishes, Pat Cone; 181, McPolin Barn, Phil Archbold; 182, Claytons Peak from Mckonkeys, Lauren Nadler; 183, Jupiter Peak Sweep, Lauren Nadler; Cover, Snow Background and All Watercolor Illustrations, Shutterstock Artists.